1

I've laughed my way through most of my life, during good times and bad, by finding the humor in almost any situation.

Many of the people I've known have given me a reason to laugh and some have had a profound and lasting influence on my life.

These stories are a collection of the best laughs I've enjoyed and the most valuable lessons I've learned.

by MJ Grady

with contributions by Diane Grady

Dedicated to
Ryan Michael Grady

Not enough laughter;
Not enough life.

Preface

Laughter has made the good times more memorable and the tough times more tolerable. My life has been a healthy and interesting mix of both times to cherish and times to forget.

During the period from seven to seventy years, I learned that life happens with or without our active participation. I've been both driver and rider during my life's journey.

The best laughs are spontaneous and the biggest lessons are unexpected. I've been both beneficiary and victim and almost every life experience has helped to shape my thinking and behavior.

Everyone has a story and most of us have many, which I believe are best when shared with others. I'm passing along the lessons I've learned and the laughs I've shared with so many people along the way.

I hope you enjoy the memories and have a good laugh either with me or on me.

Prologue

My parents met while Dad was stationed in Georgia during WWII. They settled in Buffalo, New York, where I was born and lived until the family moved to Jacksonville, Florida when I was twelve. I was embarrassingly skinny through my teenage years but have certainly exceeded my desire to change my profile.

I've never been in any danger of being awarded a Rhodes scholarship, but have thrived by working hard and living by my wits. During my growing up years, I worked at fifteen part-time jobs, including washing dishes and selling Kirby vacuum cleaners door-to-door.

After high school, I spent four years in the Air Force and squeezed in a few college courses before starting a career in the computer business. I worked for technology companies as small as three people and as large as multi-billion dollar organizations.

While working as a field engineer, sales rep and sales manager, I moved around the U.S. to nine states before settling in Seattle, when I was thirty-one. The Seattle area was my home for close to forty years and where many of the stories in this book took place.

I plowed through a few marriages before finding the love of my life, with whom I have shared close to 30 happy years. Diane was a young widow who had been raised in the Catholic faith, as I had. The Catholic Church wouldn't marry us because I was divorced but the Presbyterians were less disturbed and we were married in the Old Scotch Church in Hillsboro, Oregon.

We spent much of our married life near Seattle before building our retirement home north of Seattle on Camano Island and discovering that rural life didn't suit us. Next stop was Arizona close to where one daughter and granddaughter had already moved.

We had six children between us, and tried to find time to make them all part of our lives. The grandchildren count has hit seven, ranging in age from one year to twenty-one years. The lowest point in my life was losing my son Ryan when he was 17 months old. I don't have faith that he's in a better place, he's just gone.

The highlights of my life have been the joys that the other five have brought me as I've watched them grow into adulthood. I've been blessed with the best kids a dad could have and I love them all dearly. The happiest times in my life have been with my family, who now live in all four corners of the country. They fill the rearview mirror of my life.

Mike, Pat, Tim, Barry, Karen

Mike

Mike, '58 Ford
Mike, striped bass, Meg

Ryan
Dave, Mike

Mike, Diane
Catherine, Alison, Meg, Owen, Patricia

Elsie, Owen, Meg, Mike, Dave

Jim, Effie, Mike, Art, Diane, Vern

Mike, Ducks

Dave, Meg, Catherine, Mike, Patricia, Diane, Alison

Mike, Salmon

Mike, Steelhead

TABLE OF CONTENTS

ADULTHOOD (cont.)

CHILDHOOD

Growing up was a combination of a few years in the housing projects, grade school in one of the original burbs and my junior high and high school years adjusting to the culture of the deep south in the late 50s.

I was the firstborn of five kids in a poor Catholic blue-collar family, and spent time as a choirboy, boy scout and accordion player.

I developed a quick wit while growing up as a defense for my shyness and insecurity. I kept myself entertained with pranks and started honing my skills as a story teller and comedian.

My interest in high school was minimal, as reflected by my average grades. I was proud of my varsity letters in track and cross country, and the competition has served me well in life.

I had a few part-time jobs, including two years at *Grady's Outboard,* repairing motors and boats for Dad. I left my parents' home for the Air Force soon after I finished high school and never looked back.

I have found humor in everyday life and hope you find the following stories as interesting and funny as I did then and still do today.

Pretty Pigtails

My brothers and I attended St. Aloysius church and grade school in a suburb of Buffalo, New York from 1950 until 1956. St Al's was one of hundreds of Catholic churches and schools that were built throughout the U.S. after WWII.

Nuns were plentiful enough to staff the schools and there was a heavy emphasis on religion in every subject. The nuns there were very serious about discipline and the décor was very modest.

The desks had hinged wooden tops with a compartment for supplies and glass ink wells imbedded in the upper right hand corner. We never used the ink wells, but they fascinated me and mine provided the opportunity for my first grade school prank.

Mary was the prettiest girl in the 3rd grade, with perfect long brown pig tails, which I occasionally tugged on to gain her attention. She sat in front of me all day, every day, but hardly knew I existed.

One day, I brought water to school in my thermos and filled the inkwell with it before class. I then waited until the class of twenty kids was all quietly working on a project, while Sister Angelica paced up and down the aisles with a scowl on her face and a watchful eye on us.

When Sister Angelica's head was turned away, I grabbed one of Mary's pigtails, stuck it in the inkwell of water and announced loudly, "Hey look, there's still ink in my inkwell!"

I can still vividly remember Mary's shriek and the look on Sister Angelica's face. I remember, however, very little about the conference the principal had with Mom and me the next day.

My Brother's Boots

My brother, Pat, was two years younger than me and we walked to and from grade school together every day. It was my responsibility to drop Pat off and pick him up at his classroom.

On one particularly cold day in December, with about two feet of snow on the ground, school let out an hour early. I stopped by Pat's class, in a hurry to get home and observed his teacher, Sister Agnus, struggling to get Pat's boots on his feet.

Her face was etched with an "I'm glad he's the last kid look." After what seemed like more than a few minutes, the boots were in place and Pat stood up. As Sister Agnus reached for his coat, Pat told her, "These aren't my boots."

She sat him back down and struggled mightily to remove his boots. Beads of sweat covered her face by the time she was finished. Pat then announced, "They're my brother's boots. My mom made me wear them today because I couldn't find mine."

When Sister Agnus started muttering under her breath, I backed out of the room and out of sight. Pat emerged soon with boots, coat and mittens in place and we trudged home. Sister Agnus is probably still muttering to herself to this day.

It was so cold, I saw a dog stuck to a fire hydrant.

Smoking Squeezebox

Insisting that I test my creative capabilities, my parents signed me up for accordion lessons when I was ten years old. Dad dragged me kicking and screaming to the weekly sessions and Mom kept track of my practice times in a log book, marked with an 'X' for every 30-minute practice session.

One particularly warm summer evening, my parents were sitting on the front porch, or stoop as it was called, each puffing on a Chesterfield cigarette. I was sitting in the small den, tapping out fractured tunes on my squeezebox.

I thought it would be a great time to try my first cigarette, so I snuck into the kitchen, retrieved a cigarette and matchbook and returned to the den. I lit up, coughed and sputtered, and continued with my practice session.

When I heard the front screen door open and close, I dropped the lit cigarette next to me where it landed in a magazine rack. As the smoke rose, I squeezed that accordion harder and faster and beads of sweat starting appearing on my brow.

Mom entered the den to see her sweaty and scared son almost completely engulfed in billowing white smoke.

In response to Mom's screams, Dad ran in and quickly extinguished the smoking magazine rack.

I was sent to my bedroom, with a "What in the hell were you thinking?" look from Dad, and a promise to be dealt with appropriately later. Dad kept his promise and I stayed away from cigarettes for several years.

Good judgment comes from experience, which comes from bad judgement.

Long Distance Trouble

My dad, Owen, was born in Buffalo, and after 37 years had had enough snow and cold weather to last a lifetime. He and my mom, Elsie, who was originally from Macon, Georgia, were ready for a change. Florida seemed like a good place to start a new life with their four kids.

Dad made his first 1,100 mile trip in a Greyhound bus, armed with want ads from the last four Florida Times Sunday newspapers he had ordered by mail. It was a long weekend in that bus, but he arrived in downtown Jacksonville in the summer of 1956 with a heart full of hope.

On Monday morning Dad started answering Help Wanted ads in person. Mom called his employer, where he operated a printing press, and reported that Dad would be out sick for the day.

This routine continued each morning for the rest of the week. Mom showed my siblings and me a map of Florida every day after school and the excitement built as our nights were filled with dreams about sunshine and beaches.

On Thursday night Dad called us long distance to report that he had found a job and would be on a bus headed home on Saturday morning. My brothers and I each got to talk with him for about two minutes.

On Friday afternoon, the phone rang and my brother Pat picked up the black receiver sitting on the kitchen counter, hoping to hear Dad's voice again. Instead, the caller identified himself as Dad's boss and asked how Dad was feeling.

"He's feeling fine," Pat replied. "We all talked to him on the phone last night. He's in Florida looking for a job."

Mom heard the phone ring from the backyard and arrived in the kitchen just in time to hear Pat say "Goodbye."

When Dad arrived at work on Monday morning, he was met by his boss who fired him before he could punch his timecard.

Look 'em in the eye and lie with integrity.

Welcome to Florida

After losing his job, my parents sold our home and we were on our way to a new life. Dad drove, Mom held my sister in her lap most of the way and my two brothers and I spent our time fighting for a larger share of the back seat.

After four days and three nights on the road, the "Welcome to Florida" billboard was more than a welcome sight. It had been a less-than-peaceful trip for the six of us packed into our small 1952 Dodge coupe.

Dad pulled into the parking lot and our family filed into the welcome station, greeted by stacks of colorful brochures and the sweet smell of freshly-squeezed orange juice.

The large "All you can drink for $1.00" sign invited us to the counter as Dad produced four quarters and asked for a pitcher and six cups. We emptied the pitcher quickly and Dad asked for another round.

The pitcher was quickly filled, just as quickly emptied and Dad asked for another refill. He was told two pitchers was the limit.

"The sign says, all you can drink for a buck," Dad insisted. The counter attendant smiled and replied, "That is all you can drink for a buck."

Speed Song

My accordion lessons continued for the next few years, with only a short lapse when the family moved to Florida. I played in the instructors' band, which was comprised of one piano and twelve accordions. Band participation was mandatory for anyone taking lessons from this instructor.

The instructor held an annual recital for the parents of the band members, which included a solo number by each band member. At one particularly forgettable performance, I completely botched my solo as well as another song.

On the drive home, Dad asked me why I had stopped playing in the middle of one of the songs. He didn't understand why I had forgotten the last half of a number that he had heard me regularly practice.

I responded, "I did know the whole song. I just finished before everyone else." Thankfully, for me and for the band, that was my last recital.

Rise and Shine

We had been settled in our new home in a small suburb on the south side of Jacksonville, Florida for about a year when we were first awakened to the sound of a crowing rooster at zero dark thirty in the morning.

Later that day we discovered that our new neighbors, who had recently moved from a small family farm, had acquired a few hens and a rooster.

Dad had a few conversations with our new neighbor about the early morning crowing, but the rooster continued annoying my parents with its pre-dawn serenade.

My brothers and I heard Mom mutter under her breath one day, "I wouldn't mind if that rooster died," which my brother Pat interpreted as a license to kill.

He soon hatched a plan with Tim, our younger brother, to lure the rooster out of our neighbor's yard and into our yard. After school one day, they opened the neighbors' backyard gate and started dropping corn meal on the ground, down a short fence line to our backyard gate.

Within a few minutes, the rooster and one hen were pecking their way through the open gate, where my brothers were crouched behind the house corner, with a bucket of water at their side.

11

I didn't witness the two fowl being grabbed by the neck and drowned in the bucket, but I learned later that there was plenty of squawking and flying feathers.

My brothers then took their fresh kill behind the toolshed in our backyard. The birds were plucked, cleaned and wrapped in tin foil, then stashed in the freezer section of a small refrigerator on our back porch.

Later that afternoon, the 16-year-old neighbor girl rang our front door bell. She was a plump girl with flaming red hair and a frown on her face. Mom opened the door and was asked if she knew anything about a missing rooster and hen.

Mom called my two brothers and me into the living room and asked us about the birds, which we all claimed we hadn't seen.

Our younger sister, Karen, walked in from the den and said, "They're in the refrigerator."

Mom quickly checked the kitchen refrigerator and found nothing suspicious. She returned to the front door to report to our neighbor that we did not have her chickens.

My ever-helpful sister then told Mom to check the back porch refrigerator, which Mom did. Mom saw nothing suspicious until she opened the freezer door and found two tin foil packages sitting beside her neatly stacked clear plastic containers of frozen leftovers.

Mom called my brothers and me out to the porch and asked, "What are these?" Pat replied, with a sheepish grin on his face, "That noisy rooster you said we should kill."

By now, the neighbor girl on our front porch was getting suspicious about the delay and called out to Mom, "Have you found my chickens?" Mom returned to the living room with two tin foil packages in her hands.

"Tell me those aren't my chickens," the girl said, as very large tears started streaming down her chubby, freckled cheeks. "I think they are," Mom replied as she opened the front door to hand the red headed girl the two packages.

Mom managed a weak "I'm sorry" and closed the front door, while a very sad girl stood there crying on our porch. Mom turned to us and promised that we would talk about this with Dad when he came home from work.

The conversation with Dad was not pleasant. My brothers made restitution for the chickens by doing yard work for our neighbor for a week.

It was quiet the next morning, and every morning after that. Our neighbors moved back to a country farm later that year.

The early bird gets the worm, but the second mouse gets the cheese.

First Cigar

Dad always kept a box of cigarillos on the counter for customers at his outboard business. I helped him after school for two years, repairing motors and selling boats and fishing tackle.

One afternoon, while Dad was picking up parts downtown, I thought I'd try one of the cigarillos. I huffed and puffed and inhaled for several minutes until I felt nauseous.

Dad returned to find me sitting in his office chair, with a face greener than pea soup. "You don't look too good," he said. "What's wrong?" "Not sure," I said. "It came on real sudden like."

"What do you think it could be?" Dad asked. "Probably the flu," I responded. He said, "There's a lot of that going around." He asked if I felt well enough to drive home. I said yes, and couldn't get to the car fast enough.

I was about half way home before it dawned on me. He knows! When I arrived home, Mom met me at the door with a big smile on her face. She fixed me some hot tea, and sent me to bed.

The next morning, I awoke early and felt fine. My parents commented how quickly I had recovered, but never mentioned the cigar. That was the only cigar I have ever smoked in my life.

Hear This

Study Hall in my senior year of high school should have been called playtime. There wasn't much studying taking place in that large conference room with 45 or 50 bored seniors. Passing hand-written notes was the "texting" that was done in those days.

Mrs. Cogburn did her best to maintain quiet and civility, but, in the end, she managed only to keep the noise level down to a dull roar.

She was an elderly math teacher with poor eyesight and worse hearing. There was some improvement from hearing aids that were built into the temple tips of her thick glasses.

I raised my hand one afternoon to ask for help with a math problem. She acknowledged me and I started explaining, over the din of the rest of the room, what I was having difficulty understanding.

Suddenly, I stopped talking, but kept moving my lips. A few of my classmates cast suspicious glances in my direction as Mrs. Cogburn was hurriedly removing her glasses to check the hearing aid.

Her batteries seemed to be OK, and, as she placed her glasses back over her head, I resumed talking and continued where I had left off.

My math question was almost completely drowned out by the uproar of a roomful of laughing seniors.

It took only a second for Mrs. Cogburn to realize she had been duped and she wasn't happy! It was straight to the principal's office for me.

In a very rare moment of conscience, I decided not to try to lie my way out of this one. I simply confessed my sin and accepted my punishment of three whacks on the butt from a paddle in the hands of the principal.

It's never too early to panic.

Our Way or the Highway

Like many teenagers in the "good old days", I spent my last year of high school flipping burgers and serving shakes and fries at McDonald's. Back then, an All-American special, which included a hamburger, small bag of french fries (the only size available) and a milk shake, was 49 cents.

The restaurants were very small with no indoor tables, and customers walked up to a take-out window to place their orders. We actually had to know how to put a price for each item into the cash register and count out the correct change, because computers wouldn't come along for another twenty years.

The billboard read "500 million served" then; today it's in the billions. On a particularly slow and boring afternoon, a car drove up and parked just a few yards from the window. The husband walked up to place his order while his wife waited in the car.

I was in a very mischievous mood that day and thought I'd have some fun, although I wasn't quite sure what words of wit would leap out of my mouth.

The customer asked me for two hamburgers without mustard. "I'm very sorry sir, but we're out of mustard," I replied. "Would you like them without something else?"

He paused momentarily, then turned and walked back to his wife's side of the car. She rolled her window down – yes, rolled; most cars did not have power windows.

He then repeated what I had told him about being out of mustard. She started laughing immediately, and couldn't stop.

He caught on and glared back at me with a combination of hostility and embarrassment in his eyes. Fortunately for me, he stomped around the front of the car, shook his fist at me, opened his door and sped off.

His wife looked my way and smiled as they rounded the corner out of the small parking lot. Ray Kroc, McDonald's founder, would not have been proud!

That was my last job in the restaurant business. After high school, I enlisted in the Air Force and the next grill I saw was on Kitchen Patrol duty during basic training.

ADULTHOOD

I spent four years in the Air Force after high school, including eighteen months at the USAF Academy. My country did far more to serve me during that time than I did to serve it. The AF electronics courses and the college courses I took prepared me for a career in the computer business.

I spent a short time with AT&T, then was fortunate enough to land a job in Boston with IBM. I worked for 15 different companies in 45 years, starting as a field engineer, spending several years in sales and over 20 years in various sales management positions.

I moved around the country for different jobs and lived in 9 states before settling in the Seattle area for 37 years. I ran almost one hundred 10K races and spent many hours on racquetball and basketball courts over a 30 year period. I've always loved the outdoors and have camped, hiked, fished and hunted in many of our 50 states.

I have literally laughed my way across the country, seeking excitement wherever I could find it. I hope you enjoy reading about the following tales as much as I enjoyed living them.

Serving My Country

When I enlisted in the AF and was told I'd be serving my country, I did not envision working three consecutive 16-hour days in the officer's dining hall during Basic Training.

I thought Kitchen Patrol (KP) was peeling potatoes and washing a few dishes in the enlisted men's mess hall. Instead, I pulled KP in the officer's dining room, which required a lot more sweat in the kitchen than I had expected.

There was no slacking between meals, either. When we weren't preparing food or washing dishes, our time was spent making sure the dining room was spotless.

The food line was filled with food the enlisted men only dreamed about. Most of the officers were at least cordial, if not friendly, with only an occasional new lieutenant with an attitude.

One particularly arrogant first lieutenant picked up bread at lunch one day and snapped at me, "This bread doesn't seem fresh to me." "Oh, yes sir, it's fresh all right," I responded. He insisted again that the bread seemed stale.

"No sir, it's very fresh," I replied. "It's yesterday's bread." He told me he didn't want yesterday's bread, he wanted today's bread.

I quickly retorted, "Well, Sir, if you want today's bread, you'll have to come back tomorrow!"

When he stopped glaring at me, he left the chow line and hurried off to find the sergeant in charge. The sergeant found me shortly thereafter and had several choice words to say to me about my wise guy mouth.

I tried to defend myself but the sergeant made himself very clear about how he felt about my humor. I don't remember much of what he said, but I can tell you this: six days of KP is not twice as much fun as three days of KP.

Never pass up a good chance to keep your mouth shut.

Pie Slices

A couple of new-found buddies and I were enjoying our last night of freedom, before starting college the following day at the USAF Academy.

We pulled into a pizza parlor that boasted the largest pizzas in Colorado and ordered their jumbo pie with every topping from the menu.

When our number was called, I approached the counter to retrieve our pizza. The young man behind the counter sprung a question on me that I had not expected. He asked, "Would you like your pizza cut into eight or twelve slices?"

"You had better do eight," I replied. "We could never eat twelve slices." The crowded counter area erupted in smiles and a few snickers, and everyone seemed to get the joke except the guy behind the counter.

He returned shortly with our sliced pie, which I delivered to my awaiting friends. We three did the best we could to share eight slices of pizza equally!

Last Dance

The class of 1969 arrived at the USAFA in June of 1965, to begin a rigorous 90 day basic training program, before classes started in September. For most freshmen, this was our first time being away from home and family and we were all pretty lonely.

Freshman are referred to as doolies, which is Greek for subject or slave. It was one of the kinder terms that upperclassmen used to address us, as they continually barked out commands.

On a Saturday night in September, after classes started, we freshmen got a small reprieve from our daily routine. Young women from colleges in the Denver area were bussed to the Academy to join us at the recreation hall for an evening of refreshments and dancing to juke box music.

My classmates picked their choices for the prettiest girls and danced the evening away with them. I danced once with ten different girls from the remaining co-eds. The last girl I danced with was Emily, from Colorado Women's College.

At the end of the evening, after the girls had boarded their busses for Denver dorms, the cadets gathered for a last Coke and discussion about the evening. My friends were bragging about the beautiful girls they had danced with.

Soon, one cadet chided me for dancing with only average looking girls. Another one added that none of the girls would dance with me more than once. They were all enjoying a good laugh at my expense, but I just stood there smiling.

The laughing continued until I interrupted and told everyone that I had asked each of the girls a question before asking another to dance. "What question," a cadet asked.

The question was, "Do you have a car, I replied." Their laughter increased substantially while comments were made about my lack of social skills. The group quieted immediately when I said, "Emily has a car, and she's driving down here next Saturday night with four friends."

I paused momentarily, then added, "Whichever four of you assholes treats me the best this week gets invited back to the recreation hall for another evening of burgers and dancing."

The next Saturday night was sweet revenge for me when Emily arrived with four other girls! Four of my friends, with sheepish looks on their faces, joined me in the recreation hall for an evening with the average looking co-eds.

If wishes were horses, beggars would ride; if horseshit was sweet cake, they'd eat till they died.

Liquid Dinner

Mealtime at the Academy was never fun in my freshman year. Three doolies sat at a table of ten with seven upperclassmen, who spent much of the meal asking us questions about everything from college football game scores to details about Air Force jets.

The doolies were responsible for keeping the food replenished by raising our hand for a waiter throughout the meal.

I spent one Sunday dinner attempting to answer questions that were shouted at me from every corner of the table. Not one fork full of food reached my mouth during the entire meal, and I thought I would have to return to my dormitory room hungry.

I ordered a fresh half-gallon of milk just before the meal ended. The upperclassmen were first to exit the table, leaving the freshmen to march back to the dorms single file.

Just before leaving the table, I grabbed that full carton of milk and held it straight out in front of me.

When I reached the door of the dining hall, and started the quarter mile march to the dorm, I started yelling, "Sir, I will not forget to refill the milk."

Anyone within earshot assumed I was carrying an empty carton and was being punished for a lapse in duty. About half way to the dorm, with my arm starting to ache, one of the juniors from my table approached me and yelled at me to stop.

"At ease Grady," he said quietly. "What in the hell are you doing?" I explained what I was trying to get away with. He listened, then asked, "Is that milk carton full?" I replied, "Yes, Sir!"

He laughed and complemented me on my creativeness, because he knew that I had left the dinner table hungry. "Good luck walking all the way to your dorm with that full carton of milk," he advised. "If you lower it, you'll have some explaining to do to another not-so-understanding upperclassman."

I replied, "Yes, Sir," and continued my march to the dorm with my dinner to go. The carton of milk was still cold when I arrived at my room. Milk has never tasted as good as it did on that October Sunday evening sitting at the desk in my room.

A hungry man has only one problem; a man who has enough to eat has many problems.

Groundhog Day

My first wife, Evelyn, and I spent most summer weekends at her parents' home on Cape Cod. Her parents had lived in a 250+ year-old home on five acres since before she was born.

Her dad, Roger, was quite proud of his world-class garden, filled with corn, tomatoes, squash, peas, and several long rows of green beans - his favorite vegetable. The green beans were planted at the edge of the backyard lawn, on a high spot that bordered a low-lying area.

My wife and I, along with her brother, sister, cousin and their families had all arrived early on a Friday in July for a long weekend.

During dinner, my father-in-law complained about the groundhog that had been eating its way through his prize green bean patch. He said he had been watching for the critter every evening just before sundown and was planning to seek revenge again that evening.

We finished dinner as the sun was setting and the family dispersed throughout the house. I joined Roger as he gazed out the dining room window, hoping to catch sight of his enemy.

Suddenly, he stopped looking around and whispered, "There he is!" He pointed in the direction of the bean patch.

I spotted the critter standing motionless at the end of a long row of green beans.

Roger said, "I'm going to sneak up on him and whack him with my shovel." I immediately asked how I could help. "Come on," he said. "We'll each grab a shovel and approach him from different directions, so we can't miss him!"

I followed Roger out the side door, where we found two shovels propped up against the house. He whispered to me to sneak around the house and come up over the hill from the low spot, while he tip-toed around the garage from the other direction.

We decided that whoever got there first would take the first swing. I was holding my breath as I crouched down and slowly crept up the hill. I spotted the varmint, still standing at the end of the bean patch.

I was completely unaware of the crowd of relatives, including my wife, who had gathered at the open kitchen window.

I raised my shovel high over my head as I stepped as close as I dared before I stopped. My heart was pounding as I swung that shovel with a vengeance in the direction of the critter.

Halfway through my swing, a roar of laughter could be heard coming from the kitchen window.

It was only then that I saw movement in the dim light of dusk. There were flies swirling around the animal. It was already dead!

My shovel completed the arc and that groundhog flew 25 feet across the backyard and landed on the back porch, just outside the kitchen window.

Roger appeared from around the side of the garage where he had been waiting and watching. He had a great view of the spectacle and had barely managed to control his laughter.

Roger had shot the animal with a hunting rifle earlier that afternoon, perched it up on a stick and hatched his plan to provide the family with a lifetime of laughs.

And it has! Roger has long since passed, but I suspect he's still smiling about that vision of my shovel held high above a dead groundhog.

Opossums are born dead on the side of the road.

Carpool

In my first job after leaving the Air Force, I was a bench technician at AT&T in downtown Boston. I lived in a basement apartment in Plymouth, Massachusetts with my new wife, or "victim number one," as she has been referred to as, and our daughter Meg.

We had sold my completely valueless Dodge and kept her 1958 Ford, a remnant from her teenage years, which she cherished.

Soon after moving to Plymouth, I found a three-man carpool from Plymouth to Boston that had been together for a number of years. I joined the group and we met daily for the one hour trip, with each of us alternating driving for a week at a time.

On a particularly hot July afternoon, we were returning home around 6 pm with me at the wheel, nodding off occasionally. We were close to home on Route # 3 and I was doing 65 mph with the window down to get some air in my face, while my three passengers slept.

Suddenly, I was jolted awake by the sound of scraping metal and the pressure of the roof on my shoulder. We were sliding down the highway on the roof of my overturned car.

We came to a halt about 200 feet down the highway from the spot where I had fallen asleep and we hit the guardrail. My three passengers crawled out unscathed and pulled me, with only minor injuries, from the crushed car.

We stood there speechless for a few moments, alternately checking each other for injuries and gazing at my wife's cherished '58 Ford, which was damaged beyond repair.

The passengers then wandered around in a daze, while I stood silently with my heart pounding, counting my blessings. A highway patrol car pulled up soon after and surveyed the scene quickly, making sure everyone had escaped the overturned car.

The officer approached each of us, starting with Harry, and asked what had happened. Each of the three passengers replied that they had been sleeping and couldn't offer any information.

The officer walked up to me, expecting to learn what had happened. Before he could utter a word, I stopped him cold with, "Don't look at me, I was sleeping too."

He looked at each of us again, then at the car, then blurted out to no one in particular, "Well, who the hell was driving, if all of you were sleeping?" "Oh, that would be me," I replied.

Egg Hunt

Being single between marriages meant cleaning my apartment and cooking for myself, neither of which I was very good at. Most of the time I ate fast food or something out of a can that could be heated and eaten.

One day I decided to actually try cooking a meal. I made a short list of the foods I liked, then wrote down the ingredients for each. Armed with my list and some new-found confidence, I drove to the closest supermarket.

I was wheeling my cart around the store with my list in hand, when I came upon the egg case. There was a woman bent over the case, opening and closing egg cartons, one carton at a time.

I leaned over the case and started opening and closing egg cartons also. She glanced over at me suspiciously and moved a little further away.

I moved over closer to her and whispered, "What are we looking for?" Suddenly, she was on her way with the next carton of eggs as fast as she could get them in her shopping basket!

Speed Limit

I worked second shift as a field engineer for IBM for several years in their Boston office. The job involved being dispatched to repair broken computer systems in businesses in the greater Boston area.

On Friday nights, when second shift ended at midnight, most of us headed to Mondo's bar in the north end of Boston. The north end was home to a few bars that stayed open all night. Mondo's was close to the financial district and was frequented by second shift computer operators from office buildings close by.

After a few hours of dancing and beer one Friday night, I was pretty inebriated. I poured myself into my car to start the 25 mile drive to my apartment in Holbrook, south of Boston. I had been driving in the middle lane of Route # 3 for a few minutes, when flashing lights behind me beckoned me to pull over.

Shortly after stopping, a state trooper approached my car, and with a flashlight in my eyes, asked for my license. While looking at my license, he asked, "Well, Michael, do you know why I stopped you?"

I was pretty sure he could smell alcohol and wanted to get right to the point. I responded with, "No sir, I'm pretty sure I wasn't speeding."

"No," he said. "I wouldn't call 15 mph speeding." "Well, I was trying to be real careful," was my clever response as I looked up and smiled at him. "That you were," he retorted.

That was 1971, and instead of a night in jail, the trooper let me sleep it off in the backseat of my car in an emergency pullout about 100 yards down the highway.

Thankfully, society's tolerance for drinking and driving has changed a bit since then!

Speed limits should be the starting point for negotiation.

Thinking Ahead

Almost everyone my age was raised in a home with a hall closet that collected everything that didn't seem to fit anywhere else. The vacuum was in there with rarely-worn coats and a variety of other stuff.

I'm sure that's where my parents hid our Christmas presents when we were growing up and still young enough to believe in Santa Claus.

I was visiting my parents from across the country to rest and relax after my second divorce. It seemed like a good place to "hide out" for a few days. On my second night there, Mom and I were in the living room catching up on the latest news about my siblings and their families.

She asked me to retrieve a package from the back of "the closet." I carried a large box, neatly wrapped in dusty silver paper, back to the living room.

She told me to open it, and as I peeled back the paper, I asked, "What is this?" Mom replied that it was a wedding present for me. I said, "Mom, the wedding was three years ago."

As I lifted a brand new (three year old) electric blender out of the box, Mom said, "I know, but I didn't think the marriage would last. The blender was expensive, and I wanted you to have it when you got divorced."

Again Already

I was living in Seattle after moving around the country a few times and having been divorced twice. After a few years of being single, I called my parents in Florida to tell them about my upcoming marriage #3.

Mom answered the phone and Dad listened in on an extension as I gave them the details. They listened politely for a few minutes without asking any questions. I told them they could come out a few days early and spend some time with us before the wedding.

Mom did not reply for what seemed like several minutes, but Dad finally broke the silence by saying, "It's a long way to travel, maybe we'll wait until you have a wedding closer to home."

It's been more than a pleasure, it's been a real inconvenience.

Reluctant Gift

"Stan the man unusual" was the nickname we'd tagged Stan with at work. He was bright, funny and unpredictable as hell, offering up his unique brand of entertainment regularly for the office to enjoy.

Carol was his 4th, 5th and 6th wife; while she had only been married four times, three of these unions were with Stan. I had tried on numerous occasions to sort out their children's names and parentage, but never really got beyond a cursory understanding of where they all fit in the family puzzle.

After working together for several years, I was in charge of Stan's retirement party, attended by the entire office staff. I introduced multiple employees who entertained the audience with an old fashioned roast.

The time came for presentation of a special gift, and a lot of commotion could be heard in the hallway. I delivered a few more Stan stories, but then excused myself in front of an impatient crowd to check on the noise.

In the hallway were two employees from our Portland office who were struggling to walk one of Stan's gifts, a 40 lb. turkey, into the conference room.

Mark was tugging mightily on a leash with its noose wrapped around the bird's skinny neck, while the claws that were dug into the hallway carpet were holding this formidable bird steadfast.

I grabbed the bird from behind and picked him up by the legs. With Mark holding the leash tightly, I carried that turkey into the conference room, accompanied by a torrent of loud gobbling and flying feathers.

We placed the bird in a large cardboard box, with an opening for its head and it calmed down immediately. Everyone had a good laugh while our Portland team gave the final speech to Stan.

Stan took the turkey home, where it roamed their property for several weeks in relative peace and comfort. Diane and I had dinner with Stan and Carol a few weeks later.

We learned that Stan had butchered the bird, split it in half to accommodate being roasted in both his and the neighbor's oven, and had served it to 20 guests for Thanksgiving dinner.

Reminiscing

I made several business trips to Anchorage, Alaska and occasionally stayed for a weekend of fishing.

One weekend in 1986, I joined three friends in a Cessna 206 and flew to a remote lodge called Melozi Hot Springs Lodge. It was deep in the interior of Alaska, 200 miles west of Fairbanks. We spent three days fly fishing for grayling and enjoying the outdoor wilderness.

That weekend, a mechanic named Owen was staying at the lodge and working on one of the generators. He was a quiet guy who stuck to himself and was tough to engage in conversation.

On our third and last night at the lodge, relaxing on the outside deck, Owen opened up a bit when I asked him about his life prior to moving to Alaska.

I learned that he had been married and had a son in Portland, OR, that he saw occasionally. When I asked about his ex-wife, he said that she had remarried twice but was currently divorced.

A look of peaceful calm suddenly came over Owen's face, as he gazed into the Alaska night sky, and uttered, "I know what them boys went through."

Freeway Duck

When Diane and I started dating, she was living in Portland, Oregon, 175 miles south of where I lived in Seattle. My daughter, Alison was with me on alternate weekends. Diane and I usually saw each other on opposite weekends and an occasional mid-week business trip for me to Portland.

One Friday, I left work early and started driving to Portland in time to meet Diane and her two daughters at their home for dinner. I was just starting to merge from Route 5 to Route 215 outside Portland when I noticed Diane's car ahead, merging onto Route 215 from a side street.

I had a plastic duck bill left over from a party in the center console of my car (another story). I noticed that Diane's girls, Catherine and Patricia, were in her car and decided to have some fun.

The duckbill fit over my nose and was held on my head by an elastic string. I donned the duckbill and accelerated to pull up alongside Diane's car. She did not recognize my car and assumed I was trying to cut her off. Diane pushed the accelerator to the floor.

Soon we were speeding, nearly side-by-side, on a long, wide freeway on ramp. I was looking their way hoping to get Diane's attention.

Catherine looked over, saw me and yelled, "Mom, it's Mike, and he's wearing a duckbill!" Diane glanced back, smiled at me and we both slowed down to merge onto the freeway safely.

I followed them home and exited my car, with duckbill still intact. I looked at her and asked, "How do you like my duckbill?"

Diane took one look at me and said, "It's fine, but I'm not sure I want to continue dating a man that carries a duckbill around in his car."

If you don't know where you're going, you're not lost.

Big Brother

When I was single, shopping and simple apartment chores almost always overwhelmed me. While we were dating, Diane offered to help me shop for some much-needed household items.

When we returned to my apartment, I starting opening packages and retrieved two new pillows. I removed the plastic wrap from each and starting tearing the tags off of them.

Diane stopped me and asked what I was doing. She said the labels stated clearly that it was unlawful to remove the tags. "Why not," I asked. "Do you expect the label police to show up at my apartment?"

Decisions, Decisions

As newlyweds, Diane and I struggled with our monthly bills. I had carried some debt from my single days, and finances were very tight. Once a month, we stacked up our bills on the dining room table, and sorted them by priority.

We made decisions about which bills to pay in full and which would get a partial payment. In those days before cell phones, bill collectors would call our home phone around dinner time to ask when they could expect their money.

This was a tense time for me and one bill collector in particular annoyed me more than the others. After a brief unpleasant phone discussion one evening, I promised her half the amount that was due, which was going to leave us short for some of our other bills.

She asked, "When can we expect the other half?" in a condescending tone of voice that I didn't care for. I responded by asking her if I could explain to her how we paid our bills every month. She said, "Please do!"

I told her that once a month we put all of our bills in a hat, pulled them out randomly, and paid bills until the money was gone. Any unpaid bills were left in the hat for next month.

I told her this was the only method we could devise that gave everyone we owed a fair chance to get at least some of their money. I added that her company had as good a chance as any of receiving a monthly payment.

Before I hung up on her, I shouted into the phone, "If you don't stop calling me at dinner time and giving me grief about the money we owe you, your bill won't even make it into the hat next month!"

The more times you run over a dead cat, the flatter it gets.

Expired Warranty

Diane drove an older Mercedes Benz when we were married, and traded it in for a new E-class sedan after a few years. After four years and 58,000 miles, the car had developed problems starting and was not running smoothly.

I returned it to the same dealer she had purchased the car from, and who had done all the routine service for four years.

I dropped the car off at 7am and in late morning the service technician called me at work to discuss the $4,800 estimate they had arrived at.

I was stunned at the total and asked for some details on the repairs needed. I stopped him while he was reviewing the list, and suggested that we review the bill in person.

After lunch, I drove to the dealer and sat down with the technician for a line item review of the estimate, which included replacing a faulty starter.

I reminded him that this car was a Mercedes Benz with less than 60,000 miles and told him the last starter I had replaced was in a 1957 Dodge. I told him I wanted to speak to the service manager, who joined us a few minutes later.

We went through the bill again and I told her that some of these items should be covered under warranty.

She told me that the warranty expired after 36,000 miles and that these items were all normal wear and tear. I blurted out, "Normal wear and tear for a $65,000 MB?"

She and I argued for a few minutes, with me doing most of the talking while she was becoming increasingly agitated. I finally told her that I thought the problem we were having agreeing on the bill was our inability to communicate.

She asked me why I thought we weren't communicating. I replied, "When I'm at home and about to get screwed, my wife gives me a nice big smile. You are not smiling!"

Our conversation ended abruptly. I came back later with Diane to pick up the car, after I paid $200 for the estimate and $700 for a new starter. Diane traded the MB in for a new Lexus the next day, which she drove for ten trouble-free years.

If you want nice, fresh clean oats you must pay a fair price. However, if you can be satisfied with oats that have already been through the horse, that's a little cheaper.

Party Santa

Diane, our daughter Patricia and our granddaughter Annabelle had attended an afternoon office Christmas party with me during my last year at EMC. The staff was there with their spouses and kids to enjoy refreshments and a gift exchange. The highlight of the party was Santa Clause being there for the kids.

Two years later, after being gone from the company, I received a frantic phone call one afternoon from Michelle, the receptionist. She told me that the annual family Christmas party was two days away and that their Santa-for-hire had just cancelled.

After a persuasive few minutes on the phone, she convinced me to play the role of Santa for their party. I agreed, under the condition that my identity remain anonymous.

Two days later, I snuck up the back stairs at the EMC office and met Michelle in the janitor's hall closet. She helped me don the Santa suit and escorted me downstairs to the party room where I took my seat in the Santa chair and awaited the start of the festivities.

Soon after, spouses with kids started arriving and the employees joined them from their upstairs offices.

The room was soon filled with the sounds of kids who had formed a line a few feet from me in my Santa suit.

I recognized the first girl in line, Alissa, one of the kids I had met at the party two years earlier. She stood there staring at me, simultaneously eager and anxious. I beckoned her with, "Hi Alissa, come on over and tell Santa what you want for Christmas."

She approached cautiously and whispered, "How did you know my name?" I replied, "Santa knows everyone's name."

Alissa turned to the waiting lineup of kids and shouted, "Hey everybody, this is the REAL Santa, not a fake store Santa."

I'm pretty sure I had more fun listening to their requests than the kids did giving me their wish lists!

CAREER

I've managed to put myself into career cul-de-sacs on several occasions, sometimes blindly, occasionally jumping in with both feet.

I've had many different types of bosses and have hired, fired and managed several hundred people over my twenty-year management career.

I tried to be a good mentor and help the people I managed to make progress in their careers. More than one person I hired went on to become vice president or president of other companies.

I'd like to think that some of what I taught them was helpful in their efforts. Fortunately, I've learned from some of the best in the business, and I'm forever indebted to them.

I spent a lot of time chasing the almighty dollar and plenty of time chasing the laughs that helped make it all worthwhile.

High and Low

Over a five-year period, I worked for Norman part time painting hotels on Cape Cod. He was a one-man company who hired me for big jobs and paid me by the hour.

We were doing work on a new hotel in Hyannis, which was a big job for us, but small by today's standards. The south wall of the three story hotel was porous brick and very difficult to paint.

As we stood on our scaffolding on a brisk October day, applying paint with big heavy rollers, I glanced down at the ground 25 feet below and shuddered slightly.

I looked over at Norman a few feet away and said, "Norman, what kind of insurance do you have if I get hurt?" He responded with, "No insurance; you're a part time employee."

I asked what would happen if I fell off the scaffolding, got hurt and couldn't work. Norman grinned and replied, "As long as you keep your roller on the wall when you fall, I'll pay you until you hit the ground!"

His response sounded a little cruel to me, but such was life for a part-time painter. A few minutes later, I asked about extra pay for working up so high.

When he asked me to clarify, I said "I think it's worth an extra 10% to be working on a scaffold so high off the ground." Norman told me I had a point and that he would think about it.

On Saturday, when he gave me my weekly check and handwritten timesheet, I noticed a 10% increase for the hours I had spent on the scaffolding. I was quite surprised, and gave Norman a heartfelt thanks and a handshake.

A few months later, we spent three days painting the basement of a small two story house. At $8 per hour, with no deductions, I was counting on $192, but Norman handed me a check for a little less.

When I asked about the difference, Norman responded with a question. "Remember the six hours we spent in the basement last week? I figured that was worth 10% less."

Water always seeks its own level.

Funny Forecast

Doug was the Regional VP I reported to in my first job as a sales manager. He kept close tabs on the business with a weekly conference call with me and each of his other field sales managers every Monday morning, one manager at a time.

He referred to these calls as *Make it Happen Now* and set very high expectations about the results he expected from each of us about the deals on our forecast.

He made these calls to each field office in the western U.S. from his office in southern California. The five managers from his regional staff were with him and were to assist with any action items resulting from the calls.

On one particular Monday, I had to report that of the five deals I had forecasted to close the previous week, none had closed. Doug was not happy and expressed his concern by saying, "The purpose of this call is to *Make it Happen Now*."

The following reply leapt out of my mouth immediately: "Well, I thought I would Make it Happen Now and THEN."

All the managers at the table laughed aloud, except Doug. For the next 30 minutes I was subjected to a barrage of questions about each deal, most of which I couldn't answer. That was my last ever Monday morning wisecrack.

First Car

My first car was a faded yellow 1951 Chevy automatic with black fender skirts that I bought in my senior year of high school for $75.

I hadn't seen one like it for 20 years until I was making sales calls with Ron, one of my sales reps, in Boise. Ron didn't like my tendency to "chit chat" with customers and warned me that we had a very tight schedule.

We were on a mission to deliver and retrieve paperwork and answer outstanding questions for the seven prospects and customers he had scheduled calls with that day.

Later that morning, we rounded the corner of a downtown office building. I spotted a 1951 Chevy parked at the curb and told Ron that I had owned one exactly like that years ago.

Ron commented that our next visit was with Steve, who restored cars and had recently bought the Chevy. Ron was quick to admonish me not to mention that car, for it would surely extend the conversation beyond our allotted time.

We were there to pick up a contract and be on our way. I told Ron I would stay in the lobby to make a few calls, then join him and Steve for a quick thank you.

"Perfect," Ron said, as he left for Steve's office to finish work on the contract.

Later, I stepped into Steve's office as the paperwork was being completed and thanked him for his business. We chatted briefly, then turned to leave, right on schedule.

Suddenly, I turned back to Steve and said, "I understand that '51 Chevy on the street is yours." Steve and I spent the next ten minutes swapping '51 Chevy stories.

Ron grew more perturbed by the minute and glared directly at me while pointing to his watch.

Steve and I were close to wrapping up when he added that the Chevy was in great shape overall, especially the interior. I told him that the interior in my '51was different than the interior in his car.

He asked about the difference and I replied, "When I looked into your car on the curb outside, I didn't see Connie sprawled out in the back seat."

Steve almost split a gut laughing, and was still chuckling when Ron dragged me out of his office.

I had hoped Ron might learn a lesson about building rapport with customers, but instead he didn't speak to me the rest of the day and stayed mad at me for weeks afterward.

I don't have ulcers; I'm a carrier.

Dinner for Two

I was a sales manager with a large company when we merged with a company of similar size, and comparable, sometimes overlapping, organizations around the country.

The term merge didn't quite seem to fit the situation, as manager after manager from my company was released in favor of a person in a similar position from the other company.

It was like a war zone around the country, with daily turf battles as careers hung in the balance. I was well positioned geographically, and survived the bloodbath.

I now reported to Jim, a manager from the company we had merged with. He had wanted to select another candidate for my job, but was overruled by his manager. It was a delicate relationship between us.

At one of our first regional managers meetings, Jim suggested we have a new account contest over the next quarter. He outlined a theme for the competition that had worked for him in the past.

When I asked how he would reward the winners, he said that the first place sales rep from each District in the Western U.S. would travel to San Francisco for a dinner there with him and his regional staff.

I suggested that sales reps already spent a lot of time away from their families and perhaps he could travel to each location over the next quarter and treat the winners to dinner with their spouses.

He said he thought it was important for the sales reps to meet the regional staff. I strained an already delicate relationship when I asked, "What's the second place prize, two dinners with you?"

Second place is the first loser.

Thick and Thin

Jerry weighed in at about 285, quite a few pounds heavier than his days as a guard on his college football team. He was probably the smartest manager I've ever had.

He had a reputation for being gruff and abrupt, which belied his warm heart and strong allegiance to his friends and co-workers. I referred to Jerry as a roughly hewn intellectual.

Jerry and I developed a very close relationship over several years so it was difficult for me when I resigned for a great opportunity with a fledgling start-up company.

I spent my last day with the company at it's regional headquarters, debriefing Jerry and the other staff personnel on our business.

As Jerry and I were walking down the hall on the way out of the building at the end of the day, Jerry said, "Mike, I'm going to miss you."

I replied casually that I would miss him also. Jerry reiterated, this time with a heartwarming emphasis that he was really going to miss me!

I was touched, but in the heat of the moment said, "Jerry, I'm going to miss you too. I feel so thin when I'm walking next to you."

I used to be so thin, I had to stand up twice to cast a shadow.

Chris was a gruff and difficult-to-deal with manager. "Rough around the edges" doesn't come close to describing his personality. He was feared by many and liked by only a few.

Speaking for myself, I found him aggravating to deal with, but supportive when the chips were down.

Chris scheduled quarterly forecast reviews, which were attended by up to twenty people from the regional staff. At one of these reviews, when I finished my forecast presentation, the questions changed to personnel in my organization.

I had not been asked to prepare for this section, but answered each question as best I could about the capabilities and shortcomings of every person on my district staff.

John was the sales rep assigned to our channel partners, with responsibility to help our independent sales company partners sell our products in favor of similar competitive products.

This was a challenging job for sure, made all the more difficult by the lack of talent from the person we had in that role.

When asked about John, I replied that he had some issues, but was operating under a performance improvement plan, and I had hopes that he would improve.

Chris pressed me for more details, but I responded with a few vague generalities and stressed that this personnel issue was probably best discussed privately with him and the region HR person, who was not present.

Chris raised his voice considerably, told me this was the region staff and asked me to stop beating around the bush and give him a brutal assessment of John.

I replied, in my own stern voice, "Somewhere in the state there is a village missing it's idiot, and I think I may have found him!"

For the first and only time ever I saw a broad smile on Chris's face before he almost fell out of his chair in uproarious laughter.

The region staff turned quiet, with all eyes on Chris, not sure what would happen next. When Chris finally stopped laughing, he said, "I didn't mean *that* brutal."

He needs a job checking seconds against originals on carbon copied forms.

Favorite Introduction

Over the years, I've done many presentations and spoken at many meetings.

On occasions where I've followed other speakers, I have often used this opening line: "I feel like Elizabeth Taylor's fifth husband on their honeymoon. I know what to do, I'm just not sure it's going to be that memorable."

Good enough is usually both.

Awards

First place award for **Class** in a business environment goes to Don.

When I was promoted from the field to headquarters, Don took me shopping for an appropriate corporate suit. He chose the style and color and after I was fitted, I looked at the price tag and almost dropped my teeth.

As I was putting the suit back on the rack, Don handed the salesman his credit card, gave me a heartfelt smile and handshake that brought a tear to my eye. He thanked me for the work I had done for him and congratulated me on my promotion. It doesn't get any better than that!

First place award for **Complete Lack of Class** in a business environment goes to Ken.

He was my Regional manager, working in the Portland office, and I managed his Seattle District. Ken was scheduled to be in Seattle on a Tuesday in January, for his regular weekly visit.

He scheduled a video conference with me at 5 pm on Monday, the day before. Ken fired me on that video conference, rather than face me personally 15 hours later. I've never witnessed less class in all my life, in or out of business. It doesn't get any worse than that!

MARRIAGE

I tried and failed at marriage a few times and usually blamed my divorces on "irreconcilable differences" rather than my own shortcomings.

My current wife, Diane, has survived more years with me than my first three victims combined, through a combination of loyalty, determination and an innate ability to help us laugh our way through the occasional pain.

Fortunately, I saved the best for last, and I hope that some of my exes can say the same. I have been difficult at best and impossible to live with at worst, for much of my life.

I've spent more money in child support and alimony than I thought reasonable at the time, but it's paid off in some hilarious (at least to me) moments that are worth remembering and writing about.

Better Meatloaf

A former wife of mine made a meatloaf that I really enjoyed. One day I came home late from work and we sat down at the dinner table immediately.

She commented, "This is a new meatloaf recipe. How do you like it?" "It's OK," I said, as I asked her to pass the green beans. "What does OK mean?" she replied. "It means OK," I said.

I added, "It's fine, but I think I liked your old recipe better." "Well this recipe is easier to make," she said in a very stern voice. "Tell me if you like it or not."

I said, somewhat desperately, "It's fine; I don't think we need to have it every year, but it's fine."

It was very quiet for the remainder of dinner, and for every dinner for the rest of the week.

I've spent most of my money on wine, women and song. The rest I just wasted.

Wedding Day Jitters

It was very hot on the last Saturday of August as Diane and I paced nervously in the back room of the Old Scotch Church in Hillsboro, Oregon, waiting for our wedding ceremony to begin.

We were in our 40's and our friends and family were arriving to witness her second and my fourth marriage. There was plenty to be anxious about; we both had kids and she was selling her home in Portland to move to Seattle to join me.

I had waited until this moment, just a few minutes before the service was to begin, to give her my wedding present. She carefully removed the ribbon and paper from a package that had been beautifully wrapped by the jeweler.

Her eyes opened wide as she carefully lifted a long strand of perfect pearls out of a silver box. She asked if I would clasp them around her neck as she was too nervous.

"I understand," I said. "I'm very nervous too." "Why should you be nervous?" Diane asked with a smirk on her face. "You should have all of the words memorized by now."

My wife says I never listen to her. At least that's what I think she says.

Snowstorm and Sunshine

It was one of the worst snowstorms to hit the Pacific Northwest in years, knocking out power and snarling traffic with almost three feet of snow.

I had been in Austin, Texas for two days, in meetings with people who had ended up in my organization by virtue of a merger between our small company and two others.

At the end of the second day, I was sitting on the deck of a local restaurant with two colleagues, enjoying appetizers and 74 degree temperatures.

I called Diane to find out how she was making out with the storm that I had seen on the news. When she asked about my day, I told her I was relaxing and enjoying the sunshine.

When I asked Diane if the storm was affecting her, there was a long pause. She finally broke the silence with, "Well I'm glad you're having fun with your buddies. I'm sitting here on the floor in the den with a fire going in a cold and dark house because our electricity is out."

Diane added that the school was closed and that the students had all been sent home. She was very concerned that our girls weren't home and hadn't called. She had no idea where they were.

She also told me that she couldn't go out to look for them because the streets were too icy to drive on. "Other than that, I'm having a great day," she said. "Any more questions?"

Diane was understandably upset, near tears and was not happy about me being out of town during this crisis. I was too far away to help and had no idea what I could do from a distance.

Most phone lines were down in the area, so she couldn't contact many friends to try and locate our girls and she was understandably very concerned about their safety.

We talked for a few more minutes but there was little I could do to comfort her. We finally hung up when there was more silence than conversation.

Happily, the girls showed up at home about an hour later and she called me with the good news.

It's always darkest just before it turns completely black.

Anniversary Weekend

Stephanie Inn on the Oregon coast embodies all that you might seek in a weekend getaway, featuring romantic packages for anniversaries, birthdays and other special events in your life.

It's the perfect place for together time sans kids and pets, with champagne and roses in a room overlooking the magnificent Oregon coastline.

No detail is overlooked in providing a weekend to remember, starting with the check-in process at a small concierge desk, with a host to cater to your every need.

When I gave her our name, she said, "I see you are here for an anniversary celebration." "Yes," I said. "We're looking forward to it."

"How many wonderful years has it been," she asked. "Oh, about seventeen," I replied. Diane countered with, "Honey, it's been twenty-one years."

"That wasn't the question," I said. "Seventeen have been wonderful, three have been pretty good and one was just OK."

The host and Diane exchanged glances before Diane turned to glare at me. I thought, there aren't enough roses or bottles of champagne in all of Oregon to salvage this weekend!

Smoke Alarm

Diane and I moved into our dream home when our three daughters were all in their early teens. There were four large bedrooms with high ceilings on the upper level and two more levels below.

After about two weeks, Diane and I were awakened by a beeping sound at 2 am, and I got out of bed to investigate. It sounded like a smoke detector somewhere upstairs with a dead battery, as it chirped about every 60 seconds.

I followed the sound for several minutes, until I was confident the offending detector was in our bedroom. I retrieved the tallest ladder we had from the garage and climbed up to the highest rung to confirm my suspicion.

When it chirped one more time, I tried to twist the detector out of its socket, but it would not budge. The harder I twisted, the more frustrated I became. Diane offered, "Maybe you're not turning it the right way."

That was the last thing I wanted to hear, but I decided to climb down, move the ladder to a different smoke detector mounted on the hall ceiling. I planned to remove it from its socket, thereby verifying that I knew what I was doing. It came right out in my hand with a gentle twist.

By now, Diane was up and wondering out loud what I was doing on the ladder in the hallway. I started to explain, but then asked her to return to bed and let me finish the job. Reluctantly, she turned to make her way back to the bedroom.

I moved the ladder back to the bedroom to try and remove the defective smoke detector again. The harder I twisted, the angrier I became, as reflected by my obscene language.

Soon Diane was laughing; softly at first, but shortly the upstairs was filled with a mix of my cursing and her uproarious laughter.

Finally, the offending detector came loose in my hand and I heaved it down the stairwell, glad to be free from the chirping. It rolled down the stairs and came to rest on the landing.

By now I could see the humor in the situation and started laughing. But I was soon interrupted by another loud chirp from the smoke detector.

Diane let out a howl. I ran down the stairs, grabbed the detector and continued down to my workshop in the garage.

I grabbed my 9 pound mallet and said, "Just beep one more &(*^#@ time!" It didn't beep again, so I let it live and returned upstairs. We laughed ourselves to sleep.

Five years with me is like 5 minutes underwater.

Cold Lesson

Mount Rainer stands 14,410 feet above sea level and it's permanently snow-capped peak is visible for many miles in the vicinity around Seattle. It's a favorite destination for hikers, photographers, sightseers and mountain climbers.

I have always enjoyed the majesty of Mt. Rainier and we were fortunate enough to view it through our living room window.

During the years I lived in Seattle, several friends had climbed the mountain, and I finally decided to give it a try. My son, Dave, daughters Catherine and Alison agreed to join me.

My wife, Diane, wasn't interested in the climb, but reluctantly supported our plan to attempt the ascent with Rainier Mountaineering, Inc. (RMI), a guided expedition service.

As the mid-August date approached, Diane expressed increasing concerns to me about the adventure. During a heart-to-heart dinner conversation, she revealed that she was concerned that this climb would whet my appetite for more mountaineering adventures.

Diane knew that it was much riskier than some of the other sports I was involved in. She worried that climbing might become a new and dangerous hobby that would occupy too much of my time.

I assured her that this was a one-time only outing. She asked, "What if you don't make it to the summit of Rainier?" I promised, "Win, lose or draw, this will be my one and only climb."

The big day came and the four of us joined twenty others in a half-day class with RMI. We passed the morning class and were cleared to make the climb. That afternoon we enjoyed a pleasant hike to the 10,000 foot level and then a few hours rest at a primitive stone building called Camp Muir.

Our guides would wake us at 1:30 am and lead small groups on the climb to the summit guided by helmet headlamps. We would arrive at sunup, enjoy the view for 30 minutes and capture the event with our cameras. The sun would start melting the snow and ice enough to make a longer stay too dangerous for the descent.

By 1:30 am the building was vibrating slightly in 65 mph winds that were driving freezing rain across the mountain. The temperature outside was minus 35 degrees with the wind chill, and the visibility was near zero.

Our guide told us to get some more sleep if we could. He added that we would not be attempting a climb to the summit, but instead would wait out the storm and make the trek back down to base camp after sunrise.

At 8 am, the guides told us to prepare for the hike down the mountain. An hour later, we began the long, slow trek in the storm and arrived safely at the lodge around noon. We were a weary and disappointed foursome.

That evening, we discussed the adventure over a wonderful dinner that Diane had prepared. We all felt unfulfilled, but glad to be safe and warm.

I suggested that because we had invested in the gear and passed the training class, but were unable to attempt the climb to the summit, we should schedule another attempt the following summer.

Diane stopped me before I could continue and reminded me about the agreement that she and I had made about this climb. This was to be a one-time only event, period!

I explained that the deal we had was that if we made the summit, or tried and failed, we would not make the climb again. I added that it was never contemplated that we would not even attempt the climb to the top because of weather.

"No, the deal we had was win, lose or draw, you would climb only once," Diane snapped. "Not attempting the summit was the 'draw' part."

I sold our climbing gear soon afterward.

It's better to have loved and lost – much better.

Big Bidder

For many years, Diane and I attended a formal charity dinner auction for a hospital in Kirkland, Washington. It was a high-priced event, attended by many local executives and celebrities.

We weren't "in" with the in crowd but enjoyed the people watching and auction bidding. Over the years we were able to win a few trips, overnight stays, wine baskets and an occasional nice piece of jewelry in our price range.

At the last auction we attended before leaving Seattle, Diane and I both fell in love with a blown glass vase with six blown glass flowers. It was a tall, colorful one-of-a-kind piece of art that I decided we must own.

I hoarded our bidding money until this item was offered at the live auction after dinner. I always held back in the early bidding, hoping things would move slowly and I could jump in when the bidding was close to over.

This strategy seemed to be working for the glass vase. I raised my bid card when the bidding had slowed to a standstill and the auctioneer asked for a bid of $2300. From the far side of the room came an almost immediate bid of $2500. I waited until I heard 'last chance' and raised my card to bid $2700.

Again, my bid was answered immediately with a bid of $2900, to a cheering crowd that sensed a bidding war which would benefit the Charity.

I held back again until the last possible second and bid $3100, with Diane tugging at my sleeve and urging me to make this my last bid. I whispered confidently, "That flower vase will be adorning our mantle later this evening."

Simultaneously, I was scanning the crowd to see who was trying to steal our vase. The auctioneer called for a bid of $3300 and the enemy's card shot up immediately.

The auctioneer looked my way, asked for a bid of $3500 and I stabbed the air with my card. *We'll see who's in charge*, I thought to myself.

Within a very few seconds, my competitor's card was raised high in the air as he shouted out, "$6500!" He turned to look in my direction as the crowd let out a roaring cheer.

It was then that I managed to see through a small opening in the crowd directly into the face of Steve Ballmer, CEO of Microsoft, whose net worth was about $7 billion at that time. I'm sure that flower vase looked great on his mantle.

Never let your alligator mouth run away from your hummingbird ass.

Wrong Number

Diane executed the perfect surprise party for my 70th birthday. It had taken six months of planning, several hushed phone conversations and keeping lots of secrets from me.

The big event took place in a rented house in the suburbs of Las Vegas. The house was perfect for a large gathering and had enough bedrooms to accommodate our extended family.

Diane, Patricia, Annabelle and I made the five-hour drive in two cars, with supplies loaded in the back of each. Catherine and Alison flew in the following day and joined us.

That evening, they surprised me with tickets to David Copperfield's magic show at the MGM Grand. We had great seats and I was in my glory, as I am learning to be an amateur magician and Copperfield is one my favorites to watch.

After the show, Diane spotted a large David Copperfield cardboard cutout in the lobby, and suggested I pose for a picture.

As I stepped up next to "David" and smiled for the camera, my son, Dave, stepped out from behind and stood next to me. I couldn't believe it! He had just flown in from Boston and was standing there with a big grin on his face.

We all went out and enjoyed some late night gambling. Dave lamented that his sister, Meg, my oldest daughter, was unable to reschedule a Baltimore business event and join us in Las Vegas.

The next morning, we chose the buffet at Treasure Island for breakfast. We were in line for only a few minutes, when a familiar voice behind me asked, "How is the breakfast in this place?"

I turned around to see Meg's smiling face. What a shock. I had been fooled again, and quite easily, according to Diane. All five of our kids were together for the first time since 1991!

The conversation was loud and animated as eight of us caught up on everyone's latest news. Diane was sitting a few seats away and answered her phone mid-breakfast.

I vaguely heard her muffled responses: "Hello, no, yes, you must have the wrong number, I'll call you later." Her last comment sounded odd, but still went completely over my head.

We all spent the day visiting and catching up. Later that afternoon, Dave took me out for a two hour father and son outing. We arrived back at the house at 6 pm and opened the door to a rousing roar of SURPRISE!

The large living room was filled with family and friends that had arrived that afternoon while Dave kept me busy in Las Vegas.

I learned that the mystery phone call at breakfast had been from her brother, Jim, who flew down that day from Seattle to join the party. That was Diane's only slip in months of planning the perfect birthday for me.

Diane had ordered a catering service to set up a buffet filled with my favorite BBQ. Everyone told a story about me after dinner, making it a very special evening.

Diane had also arranged for our five kids to be together for only the second time ever, making it the biggest surprise and best birthday of my life!

She'll never top that party and I'll be on the lookout for mystery phone calls for a long time.

FAMILY FUN

It seems as though I came home from work one day and asked my wife where the "little people" were. When she asked me what I meant by little people, I told her I was talking about the shorter people that I used to see around the house occasionally. She informed me that they had all been gone for quite some time.

It just doesn't seem possible that only a few years ago we sometimes called them "yard apes", "curtain climbers" or "rug rats." Where did the time go? It wasn't that long between diapers and driving lessons, between first steps and first dates, but we managed to create a few memories and have some great laughs as the kids matured into "big people."

They are all different and all wonderful and I savor every minute that we had and continue to have with our kids and now grandkids. Here's a sampling of some of the best of times, and the biggest of laughs, from my perspective.

Halloween Treats

My first wife and I lived in an apartment complex outside Boston. It was close to Halloween and we would soon be deluged with trick-or-treaters. My wife had bought a bag of 100 Tootsie Roll pops for the occasion.

I worked the 4 pm to midnight shift for IBM and watched our two year old daughter, Meg, occasionally during the day.

Late one morning, while her mom was out shopping, Meg laid down for her daily nap and I fell asleep in a chair in the den.

While I was sleeping, Meg awoke and discovered the Tootsie Roll pops. She picked up the bag, sat down in the middle of the living room and opened it. She unwrapped her first pop, took one lick and dropped it on the shag carpet.

During the next hour or so, while I slept, Meg opened each wrapper, took one lick and dropped the Tootsie Roll pops on the carpet, where they stuck immediately.

Around noon, I was awakened by a scream from her mom, as she opened the front door. I sprang to life with a start and dashed to the living room to discover our daughter sitting in the middle of a forest of 98 white sticks standing straight up all around her.

I was laughing out loud as her mom scooped Meg off the floor and took her to the kitchen. She asked me, "What in the hell happened here?" "I'm not sure, but all is not lost," I replied. "We still have enough Tootsie Roll pops for two trick or treaters."

I slept like a baby last night; woke up every two hours with wet pants, crying.

Midair Exploring

When my children Meg and Dave were young, they used to fly from Boston to either Seattle or Tampa to meet me for vacations. They always traveled as "unescorted minors", but Meg, being three years older, was unofficially in charge during the trip.

Dave was never happy about taking orders from his big sister, but he knew that Meg would report any trouble he got into to his mom on one end or to me on the other.

On one of these trips, when Dave was about five years old, he made several trips up and down the aisle. He was intent on exploring the plane and pushing the limit of Meg's authority.

Dave entered the lavatory in the rear of the plane near the galley and emerged after a few minutes with a sanitary napkin stuck to his forehead.

A flight attendant noticed but couldn't stop him in time to prevent him marching down the aisle with a "look what I've got" look on his face. Of course, he had no idea what he had, and Meg was still too young to know herself.

The flight attendant was close behind and quickly relieved him of his prize when he arrived at his seat.

I was waiting anxiously when they landed, and the flight attendant, with Meg and Dave in tow, were the last ones off the plane.

She couldn't get the paperwork signed fast enough and made a point to tell me that Dave had been a handful. I asked if there was a particular problem that I needed to discuss with Dave. She said curtly, "Ask him!"

I questioned Dave and it didn't take me long to figure out what had happened. I only wish that I had seen it for myself.

Celebration

My son, Dave, and his fellow defensive linemen from his championship high school football team were celebrating an important Friday night win in their senior year.

He came home late, went to bed and his mom didn't see him until about noon on Saturday. Dave made his way downstairs and propped himself up at the kitchen counter. Through bloodshot eyes, he asked his mom if there was still coffee in the pot.

That was when she noticed it – the earring! She blurted out, "What in the hell is that?" "Mom, don't get excited," was all he could muster for a response.

"Don't get excited," she yelled, and quickly added, "Wait until I tell your father about this." She peppered him with more questions, but obtained very little meaningful information about his Friday night adventure.

Finally, she said, "I'm calling your father!" Dave asked, "What do you think he will do?" "He'll fly out here, take one look at that earring, and kick your ass," she yelled. "That's what he'll do!"

Dave looked at her for a brief moment and said, "I don't think he can." "That's beside the X%$& point," she screamed, as she tapped her index finger on his chest several times as hard as she could.

She did call me later that day to vent about the earring. I tried to control my laughter, and finally said, "He'll probably take it out before school on Monday; just give him a little space until then."

Dave came downstairs on Monday morning sans earring. His mom kissed him goodbye and he left for school. The hole in his ear closed soon thereafter.

New Friend

When Alison was six years old, a new family moved into the house two doors away. One of the kids that had enrolled in Alison's first grade class came home with her after school a few days later.

I came home from work one day and Alison introduced me to her new friend, Amber. She was bright-eyed, animated, and anxious to talk.

I asked Amber about her family and learned that she had four brothers and three sisters, and that her Mom was pregnant. "My goodness," I said. "That will make nine kids."

Amber was quick to tell me that her parents loved kids. I said, "Maybe they should get a TV." Amber looked at me quizzically but returned to playing with Alison. My wife told me quietly to be more careful with my comments.

When Amber returned home from her play date with Alison, her mom asked her about Alison and her family. "Alison's Dad is so funny," Amber offered. "He doesn't think we have a TV."

The next morning Amber's mom called our house and asked my wife to explain what I had meant by my "TV" comment.

Closed mouths gather no feet

Fishing Lesson

After Alison's mom and I divorced, Alison spent alternate weekends with me. In the summer, one of our favorite activities was camping and hiking in one of the many campgrounds of the Pacific Northwest.

On one of these weekends, I picked a state park near a lake for us to camp, hoping to teach Alison a little about fishing.

We rose early and left immediately for the lake where we rented a rowboat, bought some bait and asked for any tips about catching trout in the lake. The bait shop owner was very clear; no chance of catching a trout, but there were plenty of bream and crappie to be had.

We loaded our gear into the boat and I started rowing for a group of lily pads floating about a quarter mile away from the dock.

I rowed over close enough to cast next to the floating lily pads, which I thought might be a hiding place for fish. I rigged a pole with a large worm and a bobber and cast it about 15 yards from the boat.

I handed the pole to Alison and began rigging a pole for myself. Before a minute had passed, Alison turned to me and calmly said, "Dad, my bobber is gone."

I saw that her pole was bent over in an arc and that a fish was taking line out and dropped my pole immediately. I told Alison to hold on and start reeling in slowly, while keeping the rod tip up.

She did a remarkable job with her first fish ever, requiring very little help from me. After a few minutes of reeling, a large fish was visible just below the surface, hooked firmly to Alison's line. I grabbed the net and scooped a 15 inch trout into the boat.

I'm not sure which one of us was more excited. After unhooking the trout and placing it in our cooler, I started baiting our rods again.

Alison then announced, "Dad, I have to go to the bathroom." I promised that after we fished for a while longer, I would row us back to the dock. "No Dad," she said emphatically. "I need to go now!"

No amount of talking would change her mind and I started the long row back to the dock. Once there, Alison leapt out of the boat and ran down the dock toward the boat house and restroom.

The bait shop owner walked out to meet me to find out why we had come back so soon. I said the boat had gotten heavy with fish and I didn't want to capsize it.

When I opened the cooler to reveal Alison's trout, the owner was shocked. I bragged that I would row back out and catch another.

But when Alison returned from the restroom, she said she wanted no part of a return trip to the lily pads. After some unsuccessful negotiating, we returned our boat and drove back to our campsite.

That pan-fried trout was the best breakfast I had ever tasted!

When the horse is running in the right direction, let go of the reins

Christmas Memory

Diane and I purchased our first home across the street from a young family with a three year old son and a new baby. We had met Leanna and her son Tony, but didn't know them well.

That would all change on our first Christmas a few months later. It was about 9 am, the kids had opened their presents, and we were taking a coffee break when the phone rang.

Diane answered and I overheard her trying to calm Leanna, who was very distraught. She and her husband, John, had just had a huge argument. Leanna was looking for a friendly place to bring Tony and salvage Christmas morning. No better place than our home, Diane told her.

A few minutes later, Leanna and Tony were standing in our living room while we tried to clear a seat for them amidst the chaos. John had stayed at home with the new baby. Tony soon joined our kids playing with their presents.

Leanna told Diane that John had insisted that Tony have only one present for Christmas. He said that it was about the principle, not the money, and not wanting to spoil their child.

Meanwhile, Tony was flitting from toy to toy and enjoying every minute of it. He was particularly fascinated with a paint set that Patricia had just opened.

It was a set of tubes of concentrated acrylic paint and brushes. In his excitement, he knocked the black tube of paint onto our white carpet. Tony continued to inspect the rest of the set and accidently stepped on the tube on the floor.

Diane and Leanna returned to the room to see a big glob of concentrated black paint oozing out onto the carpet from under his sneaker.

Leanna let out a scream and Tony took off across the living room, leaving several black footprints on the carpet. He stopped on the wood floor in our entry and turned around to see his mom sobbing hysterically.

Leanna had come to our house to cheer up and Diane had rescued her from the brink of depression. Her son's black footprints were all over our white carpet. What a turn of events!

We three adults were on our hands and knees with paper towels, warm soapy water and my shop vacuum for the next hour or so.

Though the footprints cleaned up perfectly, the blob from the tube was more difficult. We did the best we could and Leanna scheduled a carpet cleaning service later in the week which rendered our six-month-old carpet spotless.

Like Diane had told her, no better place than our house to cheer up for Christmas.

We are pegging the fun meter now.

Joy Ride

Shortly after moving out of the rental house and into a home of our own, I traded in my sedan for the obligatory family mini-van. It was perfect for hauling kids to soccer practice and picking up stuff from Home Depot for weekend projects.

One morning, after Diane and I had taken her car out the previous evening, I got into my van to leave for work and noticed the mirror needed adjustment. Shortly thereafter, I found an empty Dairy Queen cup in the cup holder. After parking the van at work, I discovered a small dent in the rear fender.

I called Diane at home to let her know that one of the girls had taken the van for a ride while we were out the night before. Catherine was the logical choice, as she had her learner's permit and had taken several driving lessons with me.

When she returned from school that afternoon, Diane questioned her about the car, without giving her information about the clues I had found.

Of course, she denied taking the car and Diane promised a meeting with me when I returned home from work. When I arrived home, Diane and I met with Catherine in her bedroom and Diane began the interrogation anew.

Catherine broke down in tears and confessed everything. She explained how she dented the fender by backing into a chain link fence.

She told us all the places she had driven with a friend she picked up while we were out. She blubbered out quite a few stops through teary eyes.

When she finally stopped, Diane and I let her catch her breath before I asked, "What about Dairy Queen?" She started sobbing again and said, "Yes, we went there too."

There was a long pause while she composed herself and asked very calmly, "Wait a minute, how did you know about Dairy Queen?"

It was several weeks before I told her about the empty drink cup that she had left in my van!

Even though you are paranoid, they could still be out to get you.

Relaxing Weekend

A friend of mine gave Diane and me the use of their family condo a few hours from our home. It was across the street from the beach on Puget Sound and was a great weekend getaway.

Diane, Catherine, Alison, Patricia and I enjoyed a weekend beachcombing and relaxing. We were loading the Jeep for the ride home on Sunday afternoon, when I noticed that each of the girls was carrying a paper cup.

Closer inspection revealed that each cup contained a few salamanders that the girls had retrieved from the pool, just before leaving.

I insisted that, under no circumstances, were those cups of salamanders making the trip home with us. After several minutes of pleading their case, I gave in, with their promise that the creatures would remain in the covered cup.

It took only about five minutes of driving before I heard Patricia scream, "I dropped the cup." "Well, pick them up," I shot back. Patricia said, "I'm not touching those things."

I stopped the car at the first pullout, but not before the salamanders had scampered all around the inside of my Jeep. We did manage to retrieve four of the five. However, the last one died somewhere in the Jeep and was never found.

Restroom Stop

Diane and I really enjoyed tent camping with the three girls and made several weekend trips a summer while they were growing up. We usually picked state parks within a two or three hour drive of our home in Seattle.

On one trip south of Seattle, we packed up after only one night because it was a cold and wet weekend. Patricia, the youngest, was crying when we made a short stop for gas in a small town. Evidently, she was more interested in camping in the rain than sightseeing on the way home.

A few miles outside of town, Alison announced that she needed a restroom. I told her that we would wait until the next gas station. "I need to go now," Alison said. "You need to turn around and go back to that last gas station."

She then said, "I've had to go for quite a while." I asked her why she hadn't told me when we had been stopped for gas a few minutes earlier. She said, somewhat belligerently, "You should have known!"

You don't pay for your own raising until you raise your own.

Sleepover

When our daughters were in their early teens, they enjoyed having their girlfriends spend the night at our house.

One Saturday about noon, I returned home from a morning of errands to find Catherine and her friend, Emily, sitting on bar stools at the kitchen counter.

They were quite a sight with their uncombed hair in their pajamas, propped up by their elbows, trying to shake the cobwebs from a long sleepless night of movies and talking.

Catherine looked up through sleepy eyes and asked me, "What are we doing today?" I replied, with as straight a face as I could muster, "I'm going to spend the rest of the day making your lives a miserable, living hell."

Emily, who did not know me, suddenly came to life, and with trepidation in her voice, asked Catherine, "Would he do that?" Catherine answered confidently, "He might."

Her Opinion

When our three daughters were teenagers, Diane and I picked a topic once a week to discuss at the dinner table. Over the years we quizzed the girls on their knowledge and opinions on everything from abortion to gay marriage.

We wanted to encourage them to form their own opinions by debating among themselves, with questions from the parents designed only to keep the conversation moving.

We encouraged independent thinking and participation. During one of these family discussions, Patricia, the youngest, had little to say. She sat with her elbows propping up her head, staring at me, with an occasional glance at each of her older sisters.

We encouraged her to comment, but she remained steadfastly silent. Finally, I asked, "Patricia, what do you think after listening to your sister's discussion on this subject?"

She looked me straight in the eye and replied, "You sure do have a lot of nose hair!"

I have an incredible grasp for the obvious.

Undecided

Diane and I tried to pick relevant topics for our weekly family dinner discussions. These exchanges were intended to teach our kids the importance of thinking for themselves.

Our discussion on capital punishment turned out to be one of the liveliest. Diane and I discussed the death penalty in general and the alternative sentences that some states imposed for certain crimes.

I then asked our kids, "Should some crimes be categorized as so extreme that they warrant the death penalty?"

Catherine made a sound argument, that, for certain crimes, the death penalty was appropriate. Patricia nodded her agreement and said that what Catherine had said made sense to her.

Alison then explained that, occasionally, people were wrongly convicted, and she thought that "life without parole" sentences should be imposed rather than the death penalty. This sounded good to Patricia, and she changed her mind and sided with Alison.

The discussion went on for several minutes, with Catherine and Alison both making persuasive arguments, and Patricia always agreeing with the last speaker.

I intervened, and asked this question of the group, "What should be done with convicted criminals that escape from prison and commit another crime that warrants a 'life without parole' sentence?"

Patricia was quick to jump in with, "Then we should hunt them down and kill them!"

You can lead a horse to water, and he will drink if you've salted his oats.

Frightful Party

When Patricia was 15, she invited a group of friends to our home for an evening Halloween costume party. Diane and I set about to decorate the house for the occasion. We had a large front porch and thought it would be fun if I dressed up and sat in a chair on the porch as a decoration.

Thirty minutes before the party started, I donned a gorilla mask and gloves, old fatigues and hunting boots and sat in the chair while Diane sprinkled fallen maple leaves on me and the porch.

It looked as though I had been propped up there for a few days, so the plan was for me to remain motionless as guests arrived. I was completely covered, except for eye slits, which gave me a view of approaching guests.

The first to arrive was a group of three girls, two of which walked right by me and rang the bell, while the third scrutinized me suspiciously.

When the first two girls had their backs turned, I raised my hand for the third girl to see. She jumped up and down and screamed, "He's alive, he's alive!" I lowered my hand in time for the first two girls to turn, look at me and say, "You're crazy, Emily. Let's go inside." Emily kept a watchful eye on me as I winked at her through the mask.

Soon after, another girl was dropped off and walked up the porch. She stopped next to me, poked my arm and said, "Hi Mr. Gorilla." I replied, "Hi, Ms. Girl." She opened the door and rushed inside without knocking.

Soon after, Merissa showed up with her mom, Patsy, who was carrying a full silver tray of colorful cupcakes. They paid me little mind as Patsy stood next to me while Merissa rang the doorbell. I reached up, grabbed a cupcake off the tray and said, "I'll have one of these."

I had not anticipated the blood-curdling scream that I heard one second later. Patsy charged through the front door and was running around the house screaming when I came in. Diane was trying to calm her down, while I was trying not to laugh. Well, I wasn't trying that hard.

Stolen fruits are the sweetest.

Special Photo

Diane and I were attending a holiday black-tie dance one year, giving me an occasion to wear my tux, which I did not particularly enjoy.

We had finished dressing and were descending the stairs when Patricia spotted us and insisted on a picture. We poised in the living room practicing our best "smile for the camera" look while Patricia looked for Diane's camera.

Patricia arrived, positioned herself to take pictures, smiled and said, "You two look just fabulous."

I told her that I thought Mom looked fabulous in her gown, but that I felt like a penguin in my tux.

Patricia responded, "I think you're both real cute." "Cute?" I questioned. "I sure don't hear that very often." Patricia offered, "Well, I wouldn't think so."

Summer Swim

Our favorite camping destination was Lake Chelan State Park, in eastern Washington. It was a great location for early summer camping because of the variety of activities and guaranteed sunshine. There was a roped-off area for swimming, with a floating platform where swimmers gathered to sunbathe and visit.

Late in the afternoon on our first day of a trip one year, the park rangers summoned everyone out of the lake. They announced that a scuba diver had not returned to the surface with his partner and that a search party was being formed.

Through the evening and into the night, the humming of outboard engines could be heard and flashlight beams bounced off the water along the shoreline of the lake.

By morning, there were quite a few rescuers involved in the search and a rather large crowd of campers had gathered on the shoreline to watch.

Catherine and Alison decided to swim out to the floating platform at the far edge of the roped-off swimming area. They paced back and forth on the platform, hoping to get a glimpse of whatever it was the searchers were looking for.

Suddenly, they began jumping up and down, pointing at the water and started screaming, "It's an air tank, it's an air tank!"

The commotion quickly got the attention of searchers and observers. One of the state park rangers in a small boat motored over and began poking around under the floating platform.

Our girls had only calmed down slightly when the ranger stepped onto the platform and announced through his megaphone, for everyone on the beach to hear, "It's just a buoy."

That quieted the crowd and our girls, and their tears were quickly replaced with looks of humiliation. There was no place to hide, and they now had to get in the water and swim back to shore.

They went directly to their tents, followed closely by a few teen-age boys giggling, "It's just a buoy."

Spring Dance

It was Catherine's senior year of high school and time for the annual homecoming dance. Diane invited all of Catherine's friends, their dates and parents to our house for pictures before the dance.

All the couples were dressed up in sport coats and nice dresses. We served refreshments and took a lot of pictures for an hour or so before our seniors had to leave for the dance.

Shortly before the teenagers departed, I motioned Catherine's date, Matt, over to a quiet corner near the dining room table.

Smiling, I shook his hand firmly, looked him in the eye and whispered, "Any part of you that touches my daughter will not be returned."

I added, "Enjoy the dance and have Catherine home by midnight." That was the fastest I've ever seen a face turn so pale.

Deadly Afternoon

When I was 55 years old, my daughter, Alison, was in her senior year of college, studying cellular biology. She worked part-time for the pathology group at the local hospital. Her boss was also the medical examiner in this small college town.

One day at work the boss asked her if she wanted to assist him with an autopsy and she jumped at the chance. That evening, Alison called to tell me about the autopsy.

It seemed that a 55-year-old male had died suddenly. The medics who had taken him to the hospital suspected the cause, but the purpose of the autopsy was to determine the cause of death with no pre-conceived notions.

Alison described the procedure in some detail with a few questions from me sprinkled in. At one point, I said to her, "Let me see if I understand. This 55-year-old man was on the table, completely naked."

She replied in the affirmative. "And you were helping the medical examiner make incisions on various parts of his body," I stated, in an uneasy tone of voice. "Yes," Alison said. "That's how autopsies are done."

The thought of my 21 year old "baby" doing an autopsy on a naked man the same age as me was quite disconcerting. I expressed my concerns to Alison.

She tried to ease my fears by explaining why the autopsy was so important, but I was still very unnerved by the thought of what she had done.

I finally said, "This guy was my age, he was naked and dead!" Alison tried to calm me down and assured me that everything was OK.

"Dad, calm down," she said. "I promise you that we very rarely ever perform autopsies on people who are not dead."

Everybody wants to go to heaven, but nobody wants to die.

Fun Run

Diane and I flew from Seattle to Anchorage occasionally to visit Catherine. During one of our visits, Catherine took me for a long hike down a river trail that took us further away from civilization with every step.

This was a trek she had made many times, but for me it was a new adventure. While she led the way with an aggressive pace, Catherine regularly shouted out, "Hey bear!"

About thirty minutes out from the trailhead, she stopped and pointed to a pile of fresh bear scat on the trail. As the hair on the back of my neck stood up, I asked, "Is the bear coming or going?"

"No way to know," she said. "But to be safe, let's turn around and head back." When the reality that we were actually in bear country sunk in, I asked Catherine to pick up the pace, even though I was already breathing heavily.

After a few minutes, I asked Catherine how far we'd have to go to hike where there were no bears. She looked me in the eye and dryly replied, "Seattle."

Favorable Ratio

After a few years of living part-time in Alaska and traveling around the world for much of the year, Catherine enrolled in grad school at the U of A in Anchorage to study English Literature.

Spending winters in Alaska would be a new experience for her, and Catherine faced this challenge with undaunted enthusiasm.

During her first class, the professor asked each student to explain why they had chosen Alaska for their advanced studies. The answers given were unique, and Catherine was not to be outdone.

At her turn, she said, "I heard there were ten men for every woman here. I thought those were good odds. After being here for a while, I realized that the odds were good, but the goods were odd."

After three years of 90 hour weeks, Catherine received her master's degree. She had paid her own way by waiting tables in the winter and working on the summer tourist train.

Shortly after graduation, I asked her what she planned to do with this new diploma. She thought for a moment, then replied, "I think I'll hang it on the wall next to my food handler's certificate."

Chance favors the prepared mind.

Wet Rescue

With her master's degree in hand, Catherine accepted a teaching job at AVTEC, a career and vocational school for adults in Seward, Alaska.

She found a cabin to rent outside town which was located at the edge of the Resurrection River on the road leading to Exit Glacier. The cabin afforded very primitive accommodations but magnificent scenery, which was perfect for Catherine's interest in outdoor activity.

After a few months, Diane got a mid-day call from Catherine. She sounded frightened and shouted that the river was flooding, her cabin was surrounded by water and there was no help in sight.

Diane calmed her down and went into action. Her first call was to the receptionist at City offices in Seward. She explained that Catherine, and probably others, were in danger of being washed away in the river on Exit Glacier road.

It wasn't long before Diane received two phone calls. The first was from Sally the receptionist at the City office explaining that rescuers were helping people in Catherine's neighborhood.

The second was from Catherine, calling from the bucket of a front end loader that had gotten close enough to her capsizing cabin to rescue her.

She was scared and wet, but safe, thanks to some heads-up work by city personnel.

A few months later, Catherine had to go into the Seward city office to pay a parking ticket. She gave her name to Sally the receptionist and asked for help.

"Hi Catherine," Sally replied. "I talked to your mom on the phone last spring. Have you been able to move back into your cabin?" Diane had told Catherine about how Sally had helped, but now she was able to hear the rest of the story from Sally.

It wasn't funny when she was in the bucket of that front-end loader, but Catherine and Sally both enjoyed a good laugh as they reminisced.

Never test the depth of a river with both legs simultaneously.

Last Call

When she was nine years old, my granddaughter Annabelle spent a long holiday weekend at our house. At 8:15 pm on Saturday night, Annabelle came into the den to say goodnight to me.

She was very sleepy and ready for bed. I joked that, with no school tomorrow, we should stay up late, watch a movie and have some popcorn and a beer.

With a big yawn, Annabelle told me that she was too tired to stay up late. She added that her mom would not let her drink beer.

I told her that I agreed with her mom. She was much too young to drink beer but we could still stay up late to enjoy a movie and popcorn.

Then I told Annabelle we could save the beer until she was 21 years old. Annabelle replied, "Papa, you'll be dead by the time I'm 21!"

New Home

When we retired, we looked for a home in 55+ active adult communities in Arizona. Diane had researched several and narrowed her on-line search to twenty-two homes in three communities. She flew to Arizona, previewed all of these homes, and finalized a list of seven possibilities.

I flew to Phoenix to join Diane and spend two days looking at homes with a realtor before we agreed on our top two choices. They were both the same price and in the same community.

One home was newer, had no swimming pool and featured a stunning rock wall in the family room. The other was dated, had a beautiful back yard with swimming pool and a floorplan that we both liked.

We nicknamed these homes, "rock house" and "pool house", respectively. I favored the rock house but the pool house was Diane's first choice. Our daughter, Patricia, lived nearby so we asked her to join the realtor, Diane and me to visit both homes and help us decide.

As we were leaving the rock house, I pulled Patricia aside and asked for her help in "selling" this home to her mom, who favored the "pool house". She talked it up well on the drive to the "pool house", without giving away our conspiracy.

The four of us arrived at Diane's first choice in a few minutes. We walked through the front door to a stunning view of the backyard through floor to ceiling windows on the rear wall.

It took only a few seconds for Patricia to offer up loudly, "Wow, this is the house for you!"

The real estate agent and Diane smiled at each other while I scowled at Patricia. I leaned closer to her and whispered, "You sold me out. I thought you agreed to help me."

"I did," she replied. "But I can totally see you and Mom living here." As it turns out, they were both right about the house and I figured it out after living there for a few weeks.

RELATIVES

When families are blended, the resulting combination of relatives can be an eclectic group of very interesting people.

This is certainly the case with Diane and me. Our siblings, cousins, aunts and uncles come in all shapes, sizes, religions and backgrounds.

It's a colorful collection for sure. Throw in several former brothers and sisters-in-law and extended family members and you've got the makings for memorable family reunions.

More importantly, we have stories to tell about our extended family tree that still make us laugh.

Helping Hand

Diane's Aunt Evelyn and Uncle Art were favorite guests in our home for the holidays. Evelyn was a large woman with a high-pitched voice who could fill a room with her presence.

Art was quiet and shy and was likely to follow Evelyn's orders with a happy smile on his face. They were both on round two in the marriage game, getting on in years, and happy to be together.

One Thanksgiving, Evelyn and Art were visiting us in Seattle. As Diane was preparing dinner, Evelyn was watching from a kitchen bar stool. She asked Diane if there was anything she needed help with.

Diane told her that she could use some help peeling the potatoes. Evelyn swung around on her stool and yelled out to Art, who was napping in the den, "Art, get in here and peel some potatoes for Diane!"

Noisy Afternoon

Christmas could be a noisy, boisterous affair at our house when the kids were growing up. Evelyn and Art had no kids of their own and we enjoyed having them join us for the holidays. Evelyn usually invited herself anyway, and they provided some memories to laugh about.

After one Christmas dinner, one of our kids noticed an unidentifiable faint buzzing sound that couldn't be located. We all spread out around the house in search of the noise maker.

After a few minutes our daughter, Catherine, who had been following Uncle Art, shouted out, "It's Art's hearing aid!" To which Art replied, "What did you say?"

Wild Animal

Vern was an elderly neighbor who lived in our neighborhood that we met shortly after getting married. Our family "adopted" him and referred to him as Uncle Vern. We saw him often and enjoyed his helping hand and keen wit for many years.

When Vern was unable to take care of himself, his kids moved him into an assisted living home several miles north of Seattle. We visited him there as often as we could. His body was failing but his mind was sharp until the very end.

On one visit, Diane was telling Vern about an albino deer that she had spotted at the property edge of our rural home. Vern quickly asked, "Are you sure it wasn't Mike running around the yard naked?"

Duet

On another visit, I was pushing Vern in his wheelchair to the cafeteria for lunch. A notice on the door announced an upcoming special St. Patrick's Day event.

I suggested to Vern that we join the festivities, with him playing his violin and me singing "Danny Boy." Vern responded politely that we didn't have much practice time.

I told him we had three weeks, which should be plenty. "That's not anywhere near enough time," Vern replied. "I've heard you sing."

Hiding Place

Uncle Jim was always good for a laugh at holiday time and one year in particular was no exception. Our family cat had disappeared after dinner and efforts to coax her out of hiding were futile.

Diane finally assigned each family member to a room for an extensive search. After a few minutes and still no cat, Jim asked, to no one in particular, "Has anyone checked the oven?"

It doesn't take all kinds. We just happen to have all kinds.

FAMILY PETS

Introduction by Mike Grady
Stories by Diane Grady

Love me, love my pets was never truer than when Diane and I were married. She had a variety of birds, dogs and cats before we met, and we acquired a few of each in the ensuing years.

We had mixed success, which resulted in some good material for this book, and some stories which are permanent family secrets. Most of the pets provided our family with a laugh or two before they went to cat or dog heaven.

We managed to escape to our last home in the Seattle area with no pets, but have since found a dog we can live with, and vice versa, here in Arizona.

Our most interesting pet was a chicken. Yes, you read correctly; she was a cross between a Rhode Island Red and a Banty hen. And she was the most interesting pet a family could have. Our pets have trained us well and taught us how to laugh when we least expected.

Caged Fear

Pepper the cat was one of our family pets when Mike and I started dating. Mike was visiting me at my home in Portland when Pepper pulled one of her finest stunts. Mike was sitting alone in the family room where our finch, Jenny, lived in a cage on top of a six foot tall bookcase.

Pepper was sitting in the middle of the room, her tail swishing to and fro, with her eyes fixated on the small yellow bird. Mike sat for a few minutes, watching Pepper eyeing the finch. Jenny was singing softly, with no idea what was about to happen.

Suddenly, Pepper sprang through the air toward the birdcage. She clawed her way to the top of the bookcase and hung on with her front claws. Pepper peered over the edge into the eyes of the terrified bird, while dangling precariously.

Jenny was frantic as the cat struggled to get to the top of the bookcase and into the cage, and Mike was laughing hysterically.

I came into the room to check on the commotion. I would never have expected to find my cat dangling from the top of the bookcase, feathers flying from a terrified Jenny and Mike nearly in tears from laughter. Pepper dropped to the floor unhurt and Jenny died two days later.

Grilled

When Mike and I married, he was living in Seattle. I moved from Portland with my two girls and two pets, Pepper the cat and Footsie the dog, to a rental house in Kirkland, a suburb of Seattle.

One Sunday, I found an injured baby bird in the back yard which we rescued by putting it in a box and giving it water and food. Later that day, we returned it to a hiding place under a bush in the back yard where we thought it would be safe until it could survive on its own.

When Mike arrived home from work the next day, I asked him to grill hors d' oeuvres which I had placed on the wooden shelf of the barbeque grill on the back deck. He walked out to the porch to find that our cat Pepper had placed the bird, now dead, upside down on the platform, with its little feet sticking straight up in the air.

Mike was mystified and I was so busy laughing that I almost didn't notice Pepper sitting at the edge of the deck next to the house, watching the whole scene.

Soft Landing

One of our homes featured a laundry chute where dirty clothes were dropped into an opening under a sink in an upstairs bathroom and retrieved in the laundry room below.

One afternoon Patricia was playing with Pepper, chasing her around the house, when the cat ran into the bathroom. The bathroom cabinet with the laundry chute had been left open and Pepper jumped into the cabinet to hide.

Patricia followed her into the bathroom and screamed when she realized Pepper had inadvertently jumped into the laundry chute opening. I came to the rescue, opening the chute door in the laundry room downstairs to find Pepper sitting on a pile of dirty clothes.

The cat launched into the air past me, meowing loudly. When she hit the floor she ran until she was well out of sight in a safer hiding place in the back of the house. That was the last time anyone ever saw Pepper in the upstairs bathroom.

Feet First

When Pepper left us for feline heaven, Gato took her place as the family cat. All cats have the ability to right themselves during a fall from almost any height and land safely upright on their feet – *almost* all cats, that is.

I was awakened late one night to the sound of a screeching cat. Gato had fallen from an upstairs railing down to the living room floor below and was foaming at the mouth. Patricia, our youngest daughter, was awakened by the commotion and started crying at the sight of the cat in pain.

I grabbed Patricia and Gato and drove to the emergency animal clinic as fast as I could. The vet found a broken nose and gave Gato a shot for the pain but had no way to splint a cat's nose.

Mike was traveling on business and I woke him up with a call around midnight when I returned home.

Mike asked, "How much will this cost to fix?" When I replied with the answer, he asked me how much a new, hopefully smarter cat, would cost. I wasn't amused and returned home with pain meds for the cat and a large vet bill.

Gato soon healed and continued to walk that railing. She made several more flights in the air to the living room below, including once when she landed perfectly in the middle of a box of winter hats.

That cat had too many lives as far as Mike was concerned, but the rest of the family loved her. Gato was with us for a long time, until she disappeared mysteriously one night and never returned home.

Hungry Cat

Thumper was named after a pet rabbit that froze to death in a cage behind the garage one exceptionally cold winter night. We buried the rabbit, saved the cage and named a new pet cat after the rabbit.

Mike was traveling on a three day business trip when I took a very lethargic Thumper to the animal clinic. The vet found that Thumper was dehydrated, pumped water into her stomach and sent us home. Two days later, I returned to the clinic with an even sicker cat.

The vet suggested leaving Thumper for observation for a day or two. Two days later, the vet called with news that I had not expected. It seemed that Thumper had passed a two - foot piece of ribbon adorned with pink teddy bears.

She now appeared to be as healthy as ever. The vet bill was enough to buy two cats and a lifetime supply of ribbon! Sometime later, I looked over the upstairs balcony into the living room below to see a roll of ribbon spread across the living room floor, with the end in Thumpers mouth.

The cat was ingesting that ribbon like spaghetti as fast as she could. I grabbed her and started gently pulling ribbon out of her mouth. She had swallowed about two feet of ribbon. I guess ribbon is easier to catch than mice!

Party Animal

Decorations for a birthday party for one of our girls included helium - filled mylar balloons. Early the next morning the family was awakened to the sound of things being bumped into and knocked off of shelves.

I went downstairs to find Thumper running through the house with the string of one of these balloons caught in her front teeth, dragging the balloon behind her at the end of the three foot string.

The balloon was bumping into decorations on shelves throughout the house as Thumper ran from room to room desperately trying to free herself of that balloon. It was quite a sight.

I caught up with the cat and tried to remove the string from her mouth. The string was wedged between her eyetooth and the tooth next to it and wouldn't budge.

It took three of us to hold that cat still, calm her down and pry her mouth open to try and wrest the balloon from her teeth. She was not at all happy when Mike approached her mouth dentist-style with a pair of scissors in his hand.

It was only my calming effect on Thumper that made it possible for Mike to cut that string. The cat took off on a dead run for her favorite hiding place and wasn't seen again for hours.

Flying Feathers

It started one day when our daughter, Catherine, brought home a newborn chick from a wholesale plant nursery where she worked after school.

She found the baby chick wandering around lost and found evidence that the chick's mom had been killed by a raccoon. Catherine kept the newborn ball of fuzz safe in her shirt pocket until she arrived home and asked if she could keep it.

I agreed that the chick could stay until it was big enough to return to the nursery. Catherine made it a home with a cardboard box, straw, hot water bottle and a clock. She was awakened the next morning to the sound of chirping and returned from school that afternoon to find the chick had survived its first 24 hours.

A few days later, the chick had grown enough to return to the nursery and Catherine reluctantly left for work after school with the chick. Upon arriving at work, she hid the chick in a pocket of her shirt and walked around the nursery until she found a suitable place to release it. It wandered off immediately and started following customers around the nursery grounds, while chirping loudly.

A short time later there was a loud commotion on the other side of the nursery grounds. Catherine rushed over and arrived in time to save her chick from the adult chickens that were chasing it.

Her boss showed up and asked what was going on. After her tearful explanation, he replied angrily, "You can't return that chick because the other chickens will kill it. It has imprinted on you, so you are its mom. Take it home with you after work!"

Catherine came home with the baby chick and soon after, I went to her room to investigate the loud chirping. With teary eyes, Catherine told me what her boss had said about leaving her chick with the adult chickens. I agreed she could keep her new pet if she took care of it. Catherine announced at dinner that she had named the chick *Goose.*

Mike was not very excited about having a pet chicken in the family. He told us, "Well we can always put her on the grill when she grows up if it doesn't work out."

Catherine had a balcony attached to her second floor bedroom with tree limbs just a few feet away. The chick spent days in the box on the balcony and nights inside with Catherine.

Catherine was out one evening and I went upstairs to check on Goose. The box was empty!

I frantically searched the room before stepping out on the balcony. I looked around and heard a peeping sound coming from the trees. In the dim light of the moon, I spotted Goose three feet away, sitting on a limb of one of the pine trees, about 20 feet off the ground.

I ran downstairs, grabbed a flashlight, a box and a broom and hurried back to the balcony. I shined the light on Goose, reached over the deck railing, held the box under her and starting whacking at her with the broom. It must have been quite a sight, with box and broom swinging in the air, while the chick constantly chirped, avoiding attempts to knock it in the box.

I finally knocked Goose into the box with one swift swinging motion. With a sigh of relief, I returned her to Catherine's bedroom.

The next day, I told Catherine that Goose was big enough to live outside if it had a place to roost at night. There was an empty rabbit hutch on the side of the house which I thought could be used for its' home.

Mike and Catherine were in the garage on Saturday, cutting the legs off the rabbit hutch, when their neighbor, Vern, walked over to see how they were doing with the pet chicken. Mike said it was touch and go, but joked they could always eat the chicken if it didn't work out.

Vern offered, "Why don't you name it Fricassee then, instead of Goose. It probably won't answer to either anyway, and fricassee will make for a more interesting conversation when you're telling friends about the new addition to your family. And so, Goose became Fricassee the Chicken, or Frick for short.

Vern helped Catherine and Mike finish the new home for Frick, with a branch to roost, water and food dishes and plenty of straw.

Frick slept in her new cage and I let her loose in the backyard in the morning to wander around. Over the new few weeks, Frick continued to grow into a full sized hen. She must have been a combination Rhode Island Red and Banty chicken, because she was tan with a red head, but quite small for a full grown chicken.

At the end of the day, just before dark, Frick would pace back and forth on the deck along the back of the house. She pecked at the living room window to get our attention until I let her in the house. If Mike was in the family room, she jumped onto his lap and waited to be petted, while she watched TV with him.

She and Mike would cluck to each other, keeping perfect count. If Mike clucked three times, she responded with three clucks. If he clucked once, she copied him. He kept her happy stroking under her chin and on top of her little head. Frick always stared intently at the TV and we wondered if she knew what was going on.

One day Frick escaped from the back yard and was walking around in the front yard when I spotted her. I approached her slowly and attempted to herd her into the backyard. Frick would have nothing to do with that.

She had found a new playground and managed to escape my grasp every time I reached for her. I called Mike at work and he came home at noon, in his suit and tie, to find Frick pecking her way around the front yard. He approached slowly, but was no match for Frick's ability to dodge and weave one step ahead of his outreached hands.

Soon Mike was running around, dodging back and forth, trying to grab Frick. I was laughing hysterically as he chased Frick in his business suit. Mike stopped suddenly and explained, "I'm an executive. I do not have to spend my lunch hour chasing chickens. You chase the chicken, Diane. I'm going back to work."

I countered with, "I'm an executive's wife, I don't have to chase chickens either!" Mike drove off and I returned to the house. After a few minutes, I saw Frick in the back yard, happily chirping. I'm sure I saw a little grin on her beak when she looked up and saw me scowling out the window.

When Frick was five months old, she started disappearing for long periods of time during the day. She always came back to her cage in late afternoon to eat. She also continued to appear at the back window on the deck for her nightly visit indoors with the family.

One Saturday, Mike went to a shed behind the house to look for potting soil. He found Frick, clucking softly, sitting in the middle of a table, behind the shed. He lifted her up and discovered 15 brown eggs, which Frick had laid over the past 30 days. Mike called me and we inspected the eggs while Frick paced nervously back and forth, clucking louder than usual.

Mike collected the eggs and brought them into the kitchen, thinking free-range scrambled eggs sounded really good. Frick was not happy and ran around the backyard clucking frantically. I'm sure she was clucking, "Where are my eggs?"

She attempted to fly into the kitchen window a few times, but fell to the ground. I had never seen a chicken temper tantrum and it was quite a sight. Soon, Frick was running around the house until she wore herself out and went to the garage.

The next morning Frick was gone! I went to her cage in the garage to check her food and she was nowhere in sight. We searched for quite a while in the bushes around the yard. I filled her feeder in hopes she would return home and went about my daily shores.

At the end of the day, the food in her feeder was mostly gone, but Frick was nowhere in sight. Over the next several days, we searched for Frick to no avail, but her food was disappearing daily.

On Saturday, we all took turns hiding behind a big bush near the garage, with the garage door open. Soon, Catherine saw Frick walk down the side of the house and into the garage. Frick began eating her meal and clucking softly. Catherine came into the house to announce her find and everyone was excited to have Frick home.

We went to the garage, but Frick had already disappeared. Catherine told us she had first seen Frick walking along the side of the house, so maybe Frick had returned the same way and was in the neighbors' yard.

Mike called Don next door and asked if he had seen Frick. "Oh yes," he said. "We need to talk." Mike walked over and Don pointed out the poop on his front porch. He also said Frick had been eating his wife's gardenias. Don added sternly, "The chicken has to go!" Mike said he would search Don's yard for Frick and bring her home.

Mike and I searched under every bush in Don's yard until Mike called out, "Come over and check this out." Under a thick bush next to Don's house was a cache of 14 eggs. Mike and I checked the eggs, but didn't touch them.

He knocked on Don's door and reported our find. We promised to retrieve the eggs and Frick before the end of the day. Returning later with a basket, we gathered up the eggs, while looking for our runaway pet.

Soon, Frick appeared and starting running back and forth, pecking at Mike and clucking as loud as she could. She was even madder than when the first group of eggs was taken from her. Mike finally corralled Frick and locked her up in the garage that night. He was leaving for a three day trip the next morning and promised to deal with the chicken promptly upon his return. I did not like this plan!

When I approached my car the next day, I found that Frick had pooped all over the hood and top of my car and on the floor surrounding it. It was slippery! I called Mike that night and said either I go or the chicken goes. "Every time you're out of town poop happens, and this time it was slippery chicken poop," I said. Mike said he would take care of the mess when he got home. "That chicken's goose will be cooked before you get home I said," as I hung up abruptly.

The next morning I called Vern and asked him to come over and help attach chicken wire along the bottom of the wooden backyard fence. We worked diligently for several hours, lining about 200 feet of fence up to four feet off the ground.

After a lunch break, we went outside to check our work and look for places that Frick might slip through. Satisfied that our makeshift fence was chicken-proof, I retrieved Frick from the garage and let her loose in the backyard.

I was confident that the chicken wire would keep Frick in the backyard, which was big enough for her to roam. Frick wandered back and forth in the yard, confused by the new wire. She seemed to be looking for a hole to escape through, which was not to be found. I had won round one of the battle to keep Frick in our yard.

Soon, Frick headed for the middle of the yard. She rocked back and forth for a few minutes, then launched herself into the air, easily clearing the fence and landing next door. Vern and I watched in shock as my chicken wire strategy failed. How was I supposed to know that chickens could fly!

So, what was I to do now? Well, I had an idea. Molly, a friend of mine, lived on a farm and raised chickens. I called Molly and explained our dilemma and she agreed that the farm would be a good thing for Frick. Mike and I drove Frick to the farm that weekend.

Molly remarked that Frick was a cute little chicken. But when I put Frick down to run around the yard, to my horror, the other chickens attacked her. Frick could not defend herself against the much larger chickens. Molly grabbed Frick and placed her in a small coop by herself. She then added a few baby chicks from other hens to the coop. Frick was a natural mother. She loved the baby chicks and treated them like they were her own, while she continued to lay eggs.

But one day Frick became egg bound; while trying to lay an egg it got stuck! This is a very serious problem for a chicken. But Molly boiled a pot of water and held Frick over the pot to steam the egg out. Now, if I were a chicken being held over a steaming pot of boiling water, I would not be happy. Would you? But Frick seemed to know that everything would be OK. She remained calm in Molly's hands until the egg dropped into the boiling pot. Ah, what a relief!

Mike and I visited the farm a few months later to find Frick strutting around her pen with a few baby chicks tagging along behind. Molly told us that Frick had held her own against the larger chickens and had adjusted well. A few weeks later, she was just another hen roaming around the yard. Frick was soon sitting on a batch of her own eggs. When they hatched, Molly put Frick and her newborn chicks into their own cage.

Mike approached Frick and, after a few tries, managed to hold her in his hand for a few strokes under the neck. Frick looked back and forth at Mike and me and flapped her wings. Mike put her down and she scampered back to her own family. Frick was where she should be. We thanked Molly, got into our car and waved a sad goodbye as we drove down the long driveway. We both shed a tear or two on the way home.

DIANE'S HUMOR

Diane, my wife of almost 30 years, has a special sense of humor that has kept us both laughing. She will dazzle you with her smile and cut you to pieces with her sarcasm. Diane has a quick wit and will find some humor in almost any situation.

Variety is supposed to be the spice of life, but Diane's ability to make me laugh has been the spice of my life.

We love to laugh together and it's that laughter that makes the good times better and the bad times bearable.

Everyone should be blessed with a spouse that can keep them laughing as much as Diane has kept me laughing.

I hope you enjoy reading about her creative lines and stories as much as I have enjoyed remembering and writing about them.

New Name

Diane and I married each other when we were both in our early forties, she for the second time and me for the fourth. My most recent ex-wife was also named Dianne, spelled differently, but adding another layer of complication to our relationship.

One night at dinner we were discussing the challenges of starting a life together, blending families and dealing with my ex-wives.

I burst out laughing when she asked, "Should I call myself Diane Number Two or Mrs. Grady Number Four?"

Sports Fan

I was watching a football game one Sunday afternoon when I realized that I needed something from the store. I decided to leave at halftime with the score tied at 14.

On my way out the door, I told Diane to leave the game on because I would be back in a few minutes.

I returned in mid - 3rd quarter to the sound of a commercial. I asked Diane if she had kept her eye on the game.

She said, "Yes, the score is 21 to 14." When I asked her which team was ahead, she replied "Duh, 21!"

Timeout

While driving to work one Monday morning it occurred to me that I may have forgotten to turn off the propane on our grill after a cookout on Sunday afternoon.

I called Diane in a panic and asked her to check the valve, which was in a difficult position under the grill. I told her to turn the valve clockwise until it stopped.

After checking the grill, she returned to the phone to say that she wasn't sure which direction was clockwise while crouched down under the grill.

I told her to check the second hand on one of the clocks in the house to see which way it was turning. She quickly responded, "All the clocks in the house are digital."

Up and Out

After work one day, I announced at dinner that my boss had called me that afternoon and asked if I was interested in considering a position as District Sales Manager.

It was a promotion that would require moving from Seattle to Los Angeles. After a long moment of silence, I asked Diane, "What do you think?"

"I think you could have unlimited visiting privileges," she calmly responded. "Pass the green beans, please."

I used to live by the sweat of my brow, but now I live by the sweat of my Frau.

Big Speech

I was preparing a speech that I was to give as part of my emcee duties at an upcoming business meeting.

After completing my notes, I asked Diane to listen and offer suggestions that I could incorporate into my presentation.

I had just gotten started, when she stopped me and said, "Don't try to be funny, this is a serious speech." "OK," I responded. "No humor, anything else?"

"Yes," Diane said. "Don't try to sound too intelligent. Just say what you need to say." I agreed and asked, "Is that all?" "Don't try to be charming, she added. "It's not your strong suit."

By now, I was feeling pretty deflated and asked, in a somber voice, "Without humor, intelligence or charm in my presentation, what exactly should I do?"

Diane responded, "Just be yourself!"

Leather Chair

Diane and I had originally combined two households of furniture and added to it every time we moved. I had a well-worn leather chair that I rarely used and I told Diane that I thought we should give to my son, Dave.

Diane reminded me that the chair was a treasured piece of furniture from my single days and that we should keep it.

I told her that I was ready to replace the chair with something new. She asked, "Why are you in such a hurry to get rid of that chair?"

I answered, "Well, if you outlive me and re-marry, some other asshole will be sitting in my leather chair!"

Diane questioned, "Why do you think I'd marry another asshole?"

Longevity

It hasn't always been the smoothest sailing on this marriage ship. We had one of our biggest arguments a few years ago which included plenty of loud and unsavory language.

Diane made her final point by shouting, "If you don't start treating me better, I'm going to leave you!"

It took a moment for that to sink in before I responded with, "What about our wedding vows?"

She asked, "Which ones?" I quoted, "For better or worse." She countered with, "It couldn't get any worse."

I shouted, "How about until death do us part?" Diane made her point quite succinctly when she responded with, "It's taking way too long!"

Most husbands die before their wives because they want to.

MIKE'S HUMOR

None of my one-liners are original (well, maybe a few, but I can't remember which ones). Over the years, my friends and co-workers started referring to my words of wit as Grady-isms.

I've told many stories, claimed they were all true and enjoyed the laughs that have been shared with so many people I've known.

Most of them seemed to fit one situation or another, so I have been able to enjoy them over and over.

I've found a whole new audience for my sarcasm and wit here in Arizona. I hope you enjoy these as much as I do.

Feel free to use my material as if it were your very own, as I have for many years.

Favorite One-liners

It was so cold, I saw a dog stuck to a fire hydrant.

The early bird gets the worm, but the second mouse gets the cheese.

It's never too early to panic.

Never pass up a good chance to keep your mouth shut.

If wishes were horses, beggars would ride. If horse shit was sweet cake, they'd eat till they died.

If you don't know where you're going, you're not lost.

It's been more than a pleasure, it's been a real inconvenience.

It's better to have loved and lost – much better.

The more times you run over a dead cat the flatter it gets.

I used to be so thin, I had to stand up twice to cast a shadow.

I don't have ulcers, I'm a carrier.

Second place is the first loser.

If you want nice, fresh clean oats, you must pay a fair price. However, if you can be satisfied with oats that have already been through the horse, that's a little cheaper.

Closed mouths gather no feet.

He needs a job checking seconds against originals on carbon copied forms.

I've spent most of my money on wine, women and song. The rest I just wasted.

Five years with me is like 5 minutes underwater.

Most husbands die before their wives because they want to.

My wife says I never listen to her. At least that's what I think she says.

Stolen fruits are the sweetest.

Married men don't live longer than single men. It just seems longer when you're married.

I slept like a baby last night; woke up every two hours with wet pants, crying.

It's always darkest just before it turns completely black.

I have an incredible grasp for the obvious.

You can lead a horse to water, and he will drink if you've salted his oats.

We are pegging the fun meter now.

It doesn't take all kinds. We just happen to have all kinds.

I used to live by the sweat of my brow, but now I live by the sweat of my Frau.

Life is like a roll of toilet paper. The closer you get to the end, the faster it goes.

Opossums are born dead on the side of the road.

Speed limits should be the starting point for negotiation.

Even though you are paranoid, they could still be out to get you.

Soup is always cooler at the edge of the bowl.

Look 'em in the eye and lie with integrity.

Never let your alligator mouth run away from your hummingbird ass.

You don't pay for your own raising until you raise your own.

Two things happen that are signs you're getting old. First, you start to lose your memory. I forget what the second one is.

When I stepped on my new digital scale last week, the screen read, "One at a time please."

When I tried to get cash from my ATM, the paper ticket it dispensed read, "What did you do with the $100 I gave you last week?"

Words of Wisdom

Good judgment comes from experience, which comes from bad judgement.

A hungry man has only one problem. A man who has enough to eat has many problems.

Any problem that can be solved with money is not that big a problem.

Water always seeks its own level.

When the horse is running in the right direction, let go of the reins.

Chance favors the prepared mind.

Everybody wants to go to heaven, but nobody wants to die.

Be your best by being with the best.

Learn to play the hand you're dealt.

Never test the depth of a river with both legs simultaneously.

Good enough is usually both.

Random Questions

Did you save room for dessert?
I didn't even save room for the check.

What's up?
Just my weight and blood pressure.

Can you keep a secret?
Absolutely. So can I.

Why do you always answer a question with a question? *Why not?*

Is your steak cooked to your liking?
No, a good vet could save this animal.

OLD HUSBAND'S TALES

The tellers of these stories swear that they are true. I was not present for any of them, so cannot testify to their validity. But they are funny enough to be included here.

Desert Island

A friend of ours was at a party one evening when the conversation turned into a home version of the "Newlywed game." Each person would ask a question of the group, which would then be answered individually.

One person asked, "Who would you most like to be stranded on a desert island with?" Some wives looked at their husbands and said, "I'd like to hear your answer to that question."

Each husband answered with some variation of, "You dear, of course." Until it was Wayne's turn to answer, that is. "It depends," he said.

Wayne's wife, Marilyn, asked, "On what?" with a quizzical look on her face. "On how long I was going to be there," Wayne replied, rather casually. Everyone was now staring at Marilyn, wondering what her next question would be.

She asked, with a very stern tone in her voice, "What the hell does that mean?" Wayne then proceeded to explain his answer, while the rest of the husbands were bottling up laughter inside.

He said, "If it was for a weekend, I'd want Tina Turner; if it was going to be a week, I'd, of course, want it to be you dear."

After a pause he added, "However, if I was going to be stranded for several months, I'd want a woman who could pull a plow."

Be Prepared

Bob was making his first sales call on Monday morning on a new prospect named Paul. He asked Paul how his weekend had been. Paul replied, "Really good, my wife and I spent the weekend in Green Bay."

"Why Green Bay," Bob asked, as he started to laugh. "There's nothing but whores and football players there." "Is that so?" Paul snapped. "My wife is from Green Bay!" Bob was quick to respond with, "Which team did she play for?"

Appetizers

Two couples were enjoying dinner at their favorite seafood restaurant. Larry suggested that they split a dozen oysters as an appetizer.

Norm said that he didn't believe the "old wives tale" about oysters being an aphrodisiac. To emphasize his point, Norm added, "I ate six oysters last Wednesday night, and only three of them worked."

Living Well

Wayne came home one evening to find Marilyn reading a magazine. She said, "This is a very interesting article about married men living longer than single men."

She went on to describe some statistics from a long-term study recently published by the Harvard School of Medicine. Wayne commented that the article was not correct.

Marilyn told him that 100,000 married and single men were part of the study group over a period of twenty years. Wayne told her again that the statistics were wrong. Marilyn countered adamantly with, "This study was done by Harvard; it must be correct!"

Wayne offered the following explanation: "Married men don't actually live longer than single men. It just seems longer when you're married."

Life is like a roll of toilet paper. The closer you get to the end, the faster it goes.

Best Wife

Some guys I know were enjoying their regular monthly poker game one Friday night. When the discussion turned from poker to spouses, each player had a complaint about how their respective wives had changed over the years.

Until, that is, Pete announced that he had the best wife in the world. Everyone was staring at Pete, waiting for the other shoe to drop, when Charlie blurted out, "I knew someone must have gotten her!"

TAKE TWO

I've been told by more than a few people that I have a twisted, sometimes perverse, outlook on life.

I sprinkle my everyday conversations with doses of sarcasm and sometimes will be deliberately obstinate when I think it may help to make a point.

I try to encourage others to think outside the box and accept new ideas or points of view.

But mostly, I enjoy seeing people think for themselves and form their own opinions, even if vastly different from mine

.

Thanksgiving History

A twisted tale from a twisted Turkey

Pilgrims and the Wampanoag Indians are generally credited with the First Thanksgiving. It was a 3-day harvest feast that took place in Plymouth Plantation in the fall of 1621. About one hundred people celebrated with their harvest of crops and freshly killed deer and turkeys.

The Continental Congress declared the first national proclamation of Thanksgiving in 1777. The Great Seal of America, which was adopted in 1782, featured an eagle on one side.

If Benjamin Franklin had prevailed, our seal would feature a turkey instead. We might then be roasting eagles instead of the 45 million turkeys we consume annually for Thanksgiving dinners.

The terms Indian, Indigenous Peoples and Native Americans are all used today, but do not describe the diverse ethnicity of the First Americans.

During the early to mid - 19th century, settlers tried to exterminate Indian tribes by breaking treaties, killing off the buffalo herds and through western expansion - referred to as Manifest Destiny. The First Thanksgiving with Pilgrims and Indians was perhaps our last peaceful celebration together.

In July of 1863, the Battle of Gettysburg claimed 46,000 casualties, including 8,000 dead. Three months later, President Abe Lincoln issued a proclamation to designate the last Thursday of November as a day to give thanks. I guess he thought the country could use a little lift in the midst of a Civil War that would ultimately claim about 620,000 lives.

In1939, the U.S. was ten years into the great depression and the national unemployment rate was 17%. President Franklin D Roosevelt wanted to lengthen the Christmas shopping season by moving Thanksgiving from the last Thursday back to the 4th Thursday in November.

FDR probably thought that the one million unemployed people could use the extra week for Christmas shopping. He had evidently forgotten about the many football games that were scheduled on the last Thursday of November, those game dates having been set years in advance.

Only 23 of the 48 states changed Thanksgiving to FDR's new date, while 22 states stayed with the last Thursday. The other three states opted to give thanks on both of the last two Thursdays in November. Three cheers for two turkey days and states' rights!

In 1941, Congress permanently established the fourth Thursday of November as Thanksgiving Day, ensuring that dads across America could watch football all day while moms and grandmas could work all day in the kitchen.

Arlo Guthrie's 1967 song, Alice's Restaurant Massacre, told the story of his 1965 Thanksgiving dinner with Alice and her husband at a deconsecrated church in Great Barrington, Massachusetts.

It was an eighteen minute dialogue about how his arrest for littering rendered him unfit for the draft, which kept him out of the Vietnam war. Three more cheers for leftover turkey and stuffing.

Yellville, Arkansas has held a two-day Turkey Trot Festival every October since 1946. Part of the festival is their infamous Turkey Drop. Three live turkeys are dropped from low flying planes four to five times each day. Most of these birds escape into the wilderness, but a few land violently on the pavement.

One year frozen birds were dropped, probably in response to scrutiny from the FAA and various animal rights groups. Only in America can turkeys be seen falling from a plane in the sky. Is Arkansas really part of America?

It has taken pilgrims and presidents, wars and depression, football games and turkeys almost 400 years to shape one of the oldest traditions in America.

Hopefully, this Thanksgiving finds you close to the ones you love with a drumstick in one hand and the TV remote in the other.

We might also take a minute or two to give thanks for our daily blessings, for the many freedoms we enjoy in America and for those who have gone before us that made it all possible.

Gobble, Gobble!

Customer Service

Conversation with a machine

Hello, if this is a medical emergency, please hang up and dial 911. Please listen carefully, as our "impossible to understand" list of menu options has recently changed. This call may be monitored and recorded against your will for quality assurance and training purposes.

Thanks for calling our company. Your call is very, no, extremely important, so we plan to keep you waiting as long as possible, while listening to annoying music and advertisements for other products and services we'd like to sell you.

All of our customer service agents are busy helping more important customers. You may eventually talk to a human or we may exceed our time limit, hang up and ask you to call back later. Press 1 for English, 2 for Spanish and 3 if you're not sure. Please press or say your account number. I think you said AB4536DH, is that correct? No, well try again and speak more clearly.

For security purposes, please press or say the last 4 numbers of your social security number. For more security, please spell your Mother's maiden name. For even greater security, describe the universe and give two examples.

If you know your party's extension, you can press it at any time; if you'd like a company directory, press 345678, for sales press 7893456, if you're a new customer, press 46758960 and be prepared to wait for a long time, then answer the same security questions again.

For everything else, please remain on the line. We'll also ask for your home address, last 3 years' tax returns and the name of your first pet. If you're a long-time customer, you'll wait even longer while we take care of first-time customers.

If your question is really important, you may want to try our geek-designed web site. The myriad of drop-down menus and quick links will keep you confused and occupied until our phone lines free up. You can then call us again and be placed at the end of the queue.

We are experiencing an unusually high volume of calls because it's anytime of the day, any day of the week, any week of the year. Not to worry though, please continue to hold, as your call will be answered in the order that suits us, by someone eight time zones away.

Only then will you be transferred to someone who can possibly help, and you'll hear: hello, if this is a medical emergency..........

Important Perspective

e-mail from a student to her parents in the last semester of her senior year of college

Hello Mom and Dad:

Sorry I've been off line for a few weeks, but it took this long for the burns on my hands to heal enough for me to type. My jump from the dorm window caused only a minor broken ankle, which is healing well.

Fortunately, the fire was witnessed by a gas station attendant across the street who called 911 and then immediately ran over to assist me into the ambulance.

He also visited me several times in the hospital and invited me to stay with him in his apartment above the gas station while the dorm was being repaired.

His name is Al and he's a very nice man who I want you to meet soon, as we plan to get married before the baby arrives.

The baby will mean delaying my graduation, but I can always finish that later. Also, Al will need help caring for his three kids, as he will have custody of them when his divorce is final next month.

Al is not well educated, but he's ambitious and, with both of us working, we could move out of his apartment into a place big enough for the six of us in a couple of years. We may ask you for help with a down payment to make a home purchase possible sooner

Well, that's the news from here. Hope you are both doing well.

Love,
Alice

P.S. There was no fire, I am not pregnant and I do plan to graduate in June. I am, however, getting a D in French and an F in Biology, and I wanted you to receive this news in the proper perspective.

Soup is always cooler at the edge of the bowl.

FAVORITE QUOTES

"On the fields of friendly strife are sown the seeds that on other days, on other fields will bear the fruits of victory."

General Douglas MacArthur

"To give anything less than your best is to sacrifice the gift."

Steve Prefontaine

"We may have all come on different ships, but we're in the same boat now."

Martin Luther King Jr.

The following pages are a tribute to those people who had a lasting impact on me through the lessons they taught me that changed my life. These stories would be funny if they weren't so interesting and impactful.

LIFE LESSONS

Life can't always be funny. Try as we might, some things that happen in our lives do not include laughter. They are almost always unpredictable, occasionally downright distasteful, but often have a life-long effect on us.

We often don't realize the significance or importance of what we've learned until years later. Many times there is a valuable lesson in things that happen to us and sometimes there is tragedy for no reason that is apparent to us.

The following stories are meant to make you think, not laugh. Read on if you're ready for some examples of the lessons that have shaped my thinking and behavior on my life's journey.

Birthday Party

In the fifth grade, a new kid named Juan joined our class. His family had recently moved from Puerto Rico into the apartment building near our subdivision.

I told Mom about Juan, but she warned me that I should be spending my time with "my own kind". Mom had been raised in the deep south and was a bigot through and through.

Two weeks later Juan invited me to a birthday party at his home, and I rushed home after school with the news. Mom said that she would not allow me to attend a party for a Puerto Rican kid.

I told her his name was Juan, and that I was the only kid from our class that had been invited, so I was going!

Mom eventually acquiesced and sent me off with a "be careful" warning on the day of the party. She was anxiously awaiting my return when I walked through the door two hours later.

I told her I was the only white person at the party. I added that everyone was very friendly and we had a great time. Mom asked me if the Puerto Ricans celebrated birthdays the same as we did.

I told her that we played the usual games, but that something strange had happened near the end of the party.

Mom's eyes opened wide as she asked, "What happened?" "You know how we always use a spoon to eat cake and ice cream," I asked. "Well, Juan's family uses a fork."

I'm not sure if Mom was relieved or disappointed, but I was satisfied that I had made my point.

First Place Finish

We had a small but successful track team in junior high, and I was proud of my contribution to that success. It was the end of the season and we were preparing for a county-wide meet.

I had never lost a half-mile event, but I would be facing tough competition in this event, including a kid named Kevin that I had never met.

Soon after the gun sounded, I knew that it would be a grueling race. Kevin and I lead the field and he broke the tape 3 seconds ahead of me.

My coach signaled to me that I had just run my fastest time ever, but it didn't bring a smile to my face. I slowed to a walk as Kevin stopped ahead of me and turned around. I stuck my hand out to shake his and said, "Congratulations, I ran a personal best time today and you still beat me."

He smiled, looked me right in the eye and responded, "You ran a great race, pushing me harder than I've ever been pushed. I had to run my personal best to beat you."

We stood there for a long moment smiling and sweating, both of us happy with our efforts, not realizing what a valuable lesson we had learned that afternoon.

Be your best by being with the best.

Read Between the Signs

Shortly after moving from Buffalo to Jacksonville in 1956, I was with Mom on a shopping trip in a downtown department store.

As I wasn't used to the Florida heat, I was happy to spot two drinking fountains side by side around the corner. I was slurping as fast as I could when I heard a booming voice from behind me ask, "Boy, can you read?"

I turned quickly to answer, looked up at a huge man and replied quizzically, "Yes sir, I can read." "Well, read those signs then," he shot back.

I turned to find a one-word sign over each fountain, then turned to face the stranger and said, "Sir, the signs read, COLORED and WHITE."

He said, "Well then, finish your drink." I turned around and continued to drink from the 'Colored' fountain.

Again the stranger's voice boom out, "Boy, I thought you said you could read." I restated that I could read.

He then asked, "If you can read, why are you drinking from the 'Colored' fountain?" I thought momentarily and then asked, "Why not, is the water different?"

Risky Win

Coach Jerry was a hard working educator who cared deeply about the welfare of his athletes. He insisted that the track team members maintain their grades while honing their physical skills.

At the Duval County track meet, the biggest event during my senior year, I would be running the mile.

We had placed second at this meet in the previous three years. Our biggest challenge was our mile relay team, which had lost to Paxon every year.

Coach Jerry wanted this year to be different. A few minutes after completing my mile event, he asked me if I would run one leg of the four-person mile relay.

He wanted to save the quarter milers for other events where they had a better chance of first place finishes, and concede the mile relay to Paxon.

He teamed me up with three other equally slow quarter-mile runners and we practiced some basic baton passing mid-field just before the relay started.

The gun sounded and off we ran, losing ground with every step to the other six teams. Paxon's anchor man crossed the finish line to a cheering crowd of students. I was just being handed the baton to start the final lap for our team.

It was a lonely lap around the track by myself, finishing seventh of seven teams.

But our well-rested quarter milers were able to take enough first place finishes in the shorter events, that we won the Duval County meet for the first time in recent memory.

And so it is with life, sometimes you've got to take one for the team.

Learn to play the hand you're dealt.

Listen and Learn

My father, Owen, sold sporting goods at Montgomery Wards and his friend Bob sold small appliances at the same store. One evening, ten minutes from closing, they were chatting across the aisle, when a customer walked into the appliance department.

Bob asked, "How can I help you, sir?" The customer replied, "My wife sent me in here to buy your best vacuum cleaner." Bob proceeded to describe the features of his most expensive cleaner.

When the customer told Bob he was confused by all the attachments, Bob moved to a less-expensive model and repeated his sales pitch. Owen was listening and starting to rock back and forth on his heels.

In the middle of Bob's sales pitch, the customer informed Bob that he was still confused and Bob moved again to a less expensive model and started his "features" pitch.

Owen immediately walked across the aisle and interrupted with, "Sir, how can I help you?" The customer turned to Owen and said, "My wife sent me in here to buy your best vacuum cleaner."

Owen asked if he wanted to pay by check or use his Wards account. The customer handed Owen his store credit card and the paperwork was completed quickly.

Owen pointed to a door near the back of the store and asked the customer to leave via the front door and drive his car around the building to the loading dock garage door, where Owen would be waiting with his new vacuum.

The customer thanked Owen and started towards the exit, when he suddenly stopped, turned around and asked, "Which vacuum did I buy?"

"You bought the very best we sell," Owen replied. "Your wife is going to love it." The customer grinned broadly and replied, "That's great!"

By now, Bob the appliance salesman was fuming at Owen for taking a sale away from him. Owen told him he had put Bob's sales code on the paperwork.

"He didn't want to buy a vacuum, he was simply following an order from his wife," Owen told Bob. "He didn't care about features and price, just the smile on his wife's face. Don't ever confuse buying with selling."

Any problem that can be solved with money is not that big a problem

Standing Ducks

I spent my last year in the Air Force at a Missile squadron on Cape Cod, where I met Dave, who was just arriving at the base as I was being discharged.

I married a local girl and settled down on the Cape, where I took up duck hunting, which Dave had talked about doing near his home in Illinois. My favorite place to hunt was in the Great Salt Marsh near Sandy Neck Beach on the north side of the Cape.

It was a mile walk to Scorton Creek from a gravel road that ended at the edge of the marsh. The terrain was criss crossed by very small creeks and a series of irrigation ditches that had been used when salt water hay was grown and harvested there in the early part of the century.

These ditches and creeks were easy enough to jump at low tide, and only a little wider at high tide, which was usually about a foot below the surface of the marsh. But even a small mistake could render a hunter cold and wet very quickly.

I lived near the marsh and had invited Dave to join me for a day of hunting one frigid Saturday in December. He marveled at the vastness of the marsh as we made our way slowly to my favorite hunting spot in the pre - dawn hours.

The tide was low but incoming quickly, driven by the winds of a nor'easter storm that was also driving ducks into the protection of the marsh from the open water of Barnstable Bay.

By noon, the sky was dark with low clouds, the wind was blowing rain sideways and the tide had crested the creeks and ditches. The duck hunting was great, but the water had risen quickly above our ankles and concern was turning to fear.

There was nothing to do but wait out the tide and storm, but we were soon knee-deep in water with no end in sight and no way out of this vast salt water lake. We would eventually freeze to death in the cold water if we were unable to move.

After another hour, I had only a few dry inches to spare between the water and the top of my hip waders. I had stuck the barrel of my shotgun into the mud to use as a sort of crutch.

Dave had worn chest waders, so could hold out for quite a while longer, as long as the frigid water didn't render his toes immobile.

About 2 pm, we spotted a small row boat, close to the marsh edge almost a mile away. The wind drowned out our calls to the occupants, so Dave said he would walk in that direction in an attempt to gain their attention.

I told him it was suicide to try jumping countless ditches under three feet of water to get to that boat.

He said it might be suicide to stay put and added that he had some chance of making it in his chest waders, but I had none in my hip waders.

Using his shotgun as a walking stick, Dave inched his way slowly toward the boat. After what seemed like an eternity, the boat turned in our direction. I could barely make out two occupants who were rowing against a relentless wind.

Dave stood motionless while waving his arms as they moved slowly toward him. I watched from a distance as the row boat pulled up to Dave and he pointed in my direction.

He held on to the transom as he walked along slowly behind the boat, which was now being rowed in my direction.

When the boat arrived, I climbed aboard. Dave walked behind the boat as the two men rowed slowly against the wind toward the edge of the marsh. After an hour, we arrived at a small spit of land, which led to the safety of our car and home.

I've never been as cold and scared as I was that day and have never been more thankful for a friend who risked it all for me.

Over the years, I have occasionally returned to that marsh to stare out at the vastness and give silent thanks for my friends and for my life.

The following pages are a remembrance of a son gone, but not forgotten.

RYAN MICHAEL GRADY

My third wife and I had two children, Alison and Ryan. Alison lives with her family in Seattle. Ryan will forever be 17 months old. He was injured in an accident at home while I was gone with Alison. My feelings these past 37 years have swung back and forth from anger to blame and from anguish to guilt.

I will never know what actually happened to him that day. I'm left only with unanswered questions and unfulfilled dreams of a life with a son who I love and miss.

Ryan's headstone is a reminder that he is with us only in memory, but also that I am thankful for every day that we shared with each other on earth. Fortunately, several photos remain that captured him crawling, then toddling around the house.

During the last two weeks of his life, he was attended to around the clock by a dedicated team of doctors and nurses who were ever vigilant while they relentlessly pursued a solution that might save him.

The staff was kind and did their best to make us comfortable, including breaking an occasional hospital rule when they could.

The last question I was asked by a nurse was "Would you like to hold him?" "No thank you," I replied and left the room to collect my thoughts.

Hold Him

Two weeks earlier, I had spent most of the day Christmas shopping with my three year old daughter, Alison, while her mom stayed home with Ryan. It was the day after Thanksgiving and it was typical chilly and damp Seattle weather.

When Alison and I returned home around 2 pm, our long driveway was blocked near the main road with a small group of grim-faced neighbors. Alison's mom was pacing frantically.

I stopped and jumped out of the car to find a man hovered over my son, Ryan, administering CPR and mouth-to-mouth resuscitation.

Ryan's mom was too upset to tell me what had happened, only that an ambulance was on the way. I rushed to the house across the street, called the ambulance service and urged them to hurry.

After a painful few minutes, the ambulance arrived, and an EMT relieved the tiring neighbor.

Soon after, Ryan was in the ambulance headed for Children's Hospital in Seattle, with his mom and me following in a police car.

By the time we were allowed into Ryan's room in Intensive Care, he was hooked up to several monitors, with tubes and cords running in and out of every part of his body.

The attending physician escorted us into a small consultation room to explain to us that Ryan had been without oxygen for too long to stand any chance of survival.

But he agreed they would treat him aggressively until the end. And they kept their word. For the next twelve days his mom and I spent 20 + hours a day in his room, watching the incredible around-the-clock care he received from tireless and dedicated nurses and doctors.

Nevertheless, his situation deteriorated daily and we were brought into the same consultation room for several more briefings during that 12 day period.

On December 12th, we returned to the hospital after dinner at home and entered Ryan's room to find three waiting nurses. One closed the door behind us and asked his mom if she would like to hold him.

She immediately sat down in a chair next to Ryan's bed and the nurses carefully maneuvered the many cords and tubes out of the way and placed Ryan into her waiting arms.

It had been twelve days since she had held him and she gazed closely into his face at his closed eyes. After a short few minutes one of the nurses asked me, "Would you like to hold him?"

It was against hospital rules for the nurse to allow us to hold him but the doctors were on rounds and the door was closed.

The nurses knew this would be our last chance to hold him. I couldn't bear the thought of the end being so near, so I left the room with Ryan cradled in his mother's arms.

Later, my wife and I left the hospital to return home for a few hours of much needed sleep in our bed for the first time in almost two weeks.

The phone woke us up shortly after midnight.

Mike, Lobster
Mike

Diane, Mike
Dave, Alison, Mike, Catherine

Catherine, Diane, Mike, Alison, Patricia
Thumper

Frick
Frick, Mike

Diane, Julia, Mike, Debra, Dave

Catherine, Annabelle, Mike, Diane, Patricia, Alison

Ryan, Gabrielle

Meg, Dave, Diane, Annabelle, Catherine, Mike, Patricia, Alison, David

Owen, Ella
Ryan, Meg, Gabrielle

Epilogue

We've retired to an active adult community near Phoenix. Our kids live in VT, MA, AK, WA and AZ. We see them as often as we can, but it will never be often enough.

The highlight of my life was the 70th surprise birthday party Diane planned and executed to perfection. All five of our children were together with us and each other, for the first time in 25 years!

Diane and I have made great new friends here in Arizona and still try to stay in touch with our old friends. Our guest bedroom is always open for company.

We stay busy with bocce ball, team trivia and dancing. We are also part of the ambassador group, welcoming new residents to our community. Mostly, we spend time together, enjoying life and each other.

I'm learning to be a magician and enjoy performing as well as inventing new illusions. I hope to spend more time on the golf course if I can resolve chronic back and leg pain issues. Cancer and three surgeries have slowed me down but not taken me out of the game.

My first book, *Papa's Monkey*, was a collection of humorous short stories about one of my grandchildren.

Since writing that book, I have had time to reflect on the laughter that has been part of my life. There are many people that I've laughed with and that have had a positive influence on my life and the happiness I've enjoyed.

I've tried to do my best by surrounding myself with the best people possible throughout my life. I've learned wonderful lessons from many of them and tried to pass along as much of the good stuff as I could remember.

And just as importantly, I enjoy laughing at myself and my reflection in the rearview mirror of my life.

Acknowledgements

I'd like to thank my family, and especially my wife, Diane, for making the writing of this book possible. Everyone had something to add or edit and your positive feedback and encouragement kept me typing until the end.

Thanks also goes out to Irene for being available to resolve formatting issues and to Peggy, whose thoughtful criticism and input had a very positive impact on the final publication.

54352974R00124

Made in the USA
San Bernardino, CA
14 October 2017